JACK CONWAY'S WATERWAY CRUISE
BOSTON TO FORT LAUDERDALE

By

JACK CONWAY

The Christopher Publishing House
North Quincy, Mass. 02171

COPYRIGHT © 1978
BY JACK CONWAY
Library of Congress Catalog Card Number 77-99236
ISBN: 0–8158–0367–2

PRINTED IN
THE UNITED STATES OF AMERICA

With thanks to our crew, Milt Shaw, John Reardon, Frank Partsch, Ray Maher, my wife Patti, daughter Carol, and most certainly my secretary Ginnie Brett who typed and deciphered the text, most of which was written in longhand on the bridge while *Islander* was underway, and to those many, many wonderful friends we met along the 1800 miles of the waterway course, Boston to Fort Lauderdale.

CONTENTS

Phase I

Scituate Harbor to Sassafras River 15

Phase II

Sassafras River to Morehead City, North Carolina 39

Phase III

Morehead City to Swansboro 67

Phase IV

Swansboro to Charleston 83

Phase V

Charleston to Fort Lauderdale 95

LIST OF ILLUSTRATIONS

Patti waves from her new home port—the cabin of the *Islander* New River, Fort Lauderdale, Florida 2

Officers at our Scituate Harbor Yacht Club gave us the 'hand salute' as we made preparations for departure 17

The seas were churning as we 'chummed for company' on our way out of Scituate Harbor on our first day 20

Milt Shaw at the helm with the Cape Cod Canal and the Sandwich Power Station in the background 22

Snug Harbor Marina on the Jerusalem side of delightful Point Judith, our berth the first night out 23

Milt intent on his course as we come abeam *The Race* off Fisher's Island, Long Island Sound 25

The Peking, London, England, is a proud four-master thrust into the midst of the 20th Century in downtown New York City with the East River and the World Trade Towers in the background 27

Milt and I said, "rest well" to *Islander* as we left her at the Georgetown Marina on the Sassafras River 35

Dr. Bill Kermond, center, in front of his Beachcraft Bonanza on the grass strip at Georgetown with his friend Bob Hoyt, left, and Jack 38

Islander's crew for Phase II were cold but enthused as they makeready to go down the Sassafras to the Chesapeake ... 40

Ray Maher is at the helm of *Islander* as Jack points to the huge Bay Bridge which leapfrogs the Chesapeake at Annapolis .. 41

Oyster boats (Bug eyes) off-load their oyster treasure at Tilghman's Island	43
Ray and John on the bridge as *Islander* enters Norfolk Harbor	46
Liner *United States* at rest in Norfolk	47
Busy little tug and Coast Guard Cutter bustling at work in active Norfolk	48
Portsmouth Lightship now a dockside museum	50
We waited and waited for the railroad bridge to open and the long train of little trucks seemed endless	51
Views were spectacular on the Albemarle-Chesapeake Canal	55
Dockmaster James Heston was there to greet us at the Morehead City Marina	65
Milt Shaw in nautical mood as we make ready to depart from Morehead City	68
Donnie straddles our engine and his expression tells the story	75
Catching fish is big business at Swansboro	78
John checks over the charts below Swansboro	80
Frank admits it's "cold on the bridge"	87
Guardian of Frying Pan Shoals, off Shallotte Inlet gets some yard work	88
Getting across the Waterway is not always by bridge	89
Frank puts her dockside at Charleston	90
Islander waits for a new engine at winter quarters in Charleston	91
Carol's first bridge—Beaufort, S. C.	98
Isle of Hope, Georgia, is beautiful. Carol, Patti and John take a stroll	101
Islander at Isle of Hope as Jack and Patti wait for Drummond	102
Osmer Bailey bends over heat exchanger as John oversees the project	103
Drummond Farley works on the riser	104
Patti enjoys the passage of Saint Catherine's Sound between Savannah and Jacksonville	108
John and Jack watch the channel above Fernandina, Florida	109

Islander visits Jacksonville Beach as John and Carol indicate, "So what else is new?" 111
The Waterway below Marineland was magnificent 114
Carol was a great helmsman, a new security blanket 116
Now she makes the lines ready 119
The banks of Fort Lauderdale's New River are always interesting 135
The *Jungle Queen* squeezes her way up the New River several times a day 136
Jackie waits at dockside as we arrive 137
"Let's fill 'er up, Dad," says Jackie 138
Patti, Carol and Jackie 140
My nieces Denise and Jaimie Conway help Carol wash down the decks at our New River berth 141
Georgetown Marina from plane 142
Typical traffic on waterway 142

COMPASS COURSE 180°

PHASE I

SCITUATE HARBOR TO SASSAFRAS RIVER

The two of us, Milt Shaw and I, had just finished a heavy steak dinner at Dante's Inferno, an old inn at Manasquan Inlet in northern New Jersey. It was Tuesday, October 7, 1976, and we were on the fourth day of the first leg of a long-planned boat trip from Scituate to Florida along the Intracoastal Waterway.

The *Islander,* a sturdy thirty-seven-foot Egg Harbor Sports Fisherman, had performed well during some bad weather from Scituate. We stood at the window of the restaurant and looked at her tied snugly to the end of the pier at Dante's. She had good lines, a planed bow that split the sea and sent the water cascading to either side.

Her sturdy wood hull sat firmly in a heavy sea, and the lines of the flying bridge grew right out of the cabin area. This was one boat which really looked like an adventurer, which she was fast becoming. She was painted white all over, had a brightly varnished transom and some, but not too much, other varnished areas. Her afterdeck was teak and her twin Palmer 265-horsepower fresh water-cooled engines gave us plenty of power for a comfortable twelve to fourteen knot cruising speed.

A big moon had come out, and the fog and overcast started to dissipate. Milt and I looked out at this picture-postcard scene—boat, pier, shimmering moonlit inlet—and reflected on the fun and adventure we had shared in these first four days of our trip south.

The Crew

My old friend and partner, John Reardon, had originally intended to take this first leg of the trip with me, but his wife, Mary, was not feeling too well, so he cancelled out. Naturally I couldn't go alone, and when you look around at a world full of people with the responsibilities of making livings and taking care of families, it is not too easy to think of someone who would have the time, the inclination and the seafaring derring-do to undertake a long and possibly dangerous boat trip.

I was at home in Cohasset the night John had cancelled out, and I almost felt I'd have to forget the trip, but my wife Patti urged me to keep at it. "You'll think of someone—don't stop plans now, you may never have the opportunity again."

I thought for awhile, then a name flashed onto the screen of my mind! MILT SHAW!

A half-dozen years before, when I was the president of the Massachusetts Association of Realtors, Milt the executive vice president, and our good wives Patti and Blanche, were at the National Realtors Convention at Miami Beach. One night late, or I should say one morning early, El Milto and I were on the balcony of our suite at the Fountainbleau looking down on the Intracoastal.

I remember pledging to Milt that "someday I'm going to take a boat down that Intracoastal from Boston to Florida," and I remember Milt answering, "If you ever do it, count me in because I'd really like to go too."

So, I called his apartment in Boston, and, as luck would have it, he was home just getting ready to watch the first Carter-Ford debate. I said, "Milt, do you remember a conversation we had five or six years ago about 1:30 one morning on the balcony of the Fountainbleau Hotel?"

"Keep talking, Jack," he commented.

"Well, that night we talked about a trip down the Intracoastal

COMPASS COURSE 180° 17

Officers at our Scituate Harbor Yacht Club gave us the 'hand salute' as we made preparations for departure. They are, l to r, Commodore John Reardon, Vice Commodore Ed McLevedge, Rear Commodore Jack Powell, Treasurer Dick Farrell and Secretary Joe Bowker.

and you said if it was on 'go' to give you a call. Well—it's on 'go,' and I want to make the first leg of the trip next week, Scituate to the Chesapeake. How do you feel about it?"

"When are you leaving?"

"A week from Saturday—October 4th."

"Let me think about it for a minute—OK. I've thought about it and I'm ready to shove off."

So, my long-dreamed-of trip was taking firm shape and the die had been cast—Saturday, October 4, 0600 from Scituate.

Preparations

I suppose for such a long-awaited trip as this was going to be, I should have spent the next eight days preparing for various contingencies, getting a few spare parts, or lining up my courses and charts. But running our business is a time consumer and between seeing to the business, visiting my mother, who was in Winchester recovering from a difficult cancer operation, and buttoning up some of my duties at the South Shore Chamber of Commerce, of which I was serving as president, I really had little time to think about the trip.

Ed Spike at the Ship's Locker in Scituate was kind enough to get the Scituate to New York City charts, and Milt was able to find a place in Boston where he was able to buy the New York City to Norfolk charts.

Patti spent a day before the departure date cleaning the inside of *Islander*, John Reardon had Danny Lincoln change plugs and points and change the oil. John had her gassed, and I even took a few hours to lay a coat of varnish on the brightwork of the bridge.

Milt kept in touch with Patti as they made plans for provisioning, while I raced crazily pillar to post tying up the loose ends of my business life.

Patti cooked up what later seemed like pounds of chile con carne. Milt brought quarts of beef stew that Ann Jones had made.

John, always thinking of the necessaries of life, dropped by Jack Turner's and bought six cases of Miller's beer—the staff of life on a long cruise.

Saturday, October 4—Bad Weather

The day came. Milt drove down to my house in Cohasset for dinner; we were going to stay aboard that night so we could be out of the harbor by 0600.

But, boy, did that old weatherman poke his nose into our affairs, and Friday came up northeast with thirty-knot winds and rains.

As we ate dinner at Cohasset that Friday, there was little chance that we could get on our way the next day, for rain was driving like only a northeast blow can.

"Why don't you two stay here tonight?" suggested Patti. "You'll never get out tomorrow."

But there was something in this whole adventure which was a challenge, and it sure would have been a step backwards to spend the long-awaited first night of our cruise in the luxury of a warm, oil-heated, 100-year-old colonial house on Cohasset Town Green.

We had planned for thrills and adventure, so it was "Good-bye" to Patti, Carol, Jackie and Toto (our Scotty) and by 2100 we were trying in vain to get the heat going on the *Islander*. No luck! So we had a few stiff drinks, me for Turner's bourbon, Milt for a few Beefeater's and tonic. We crawled into our sleeping bags and listened to the wind howl, the rigging of the sailboats in the harbor slap wildly against their aluminum masts. We pitched. We bucked. But our cabin was dry and we went to sleep with dreams of the long-awaited passage before us.

The morning was bad. Very bad. Small craft warnings were flying from the Scituate Coast Guard Station. Winds were twenty to twenty-five knots. The sea was raging, but we felt the storm was subsiding.

John came down to the marina and took apart the heater, fixed it and checked out our squeaking generator. Some of the boys stopped by. We had fun and talked and hoped Sunday would be a better day. That night Patti, Milt, John and I had dinner at Red Richards' Satuit in Scituate Harbor and the rains continued anew—hard, driving northeasterly rain.

"Why not stay at Cohasset tonight?" Patti again offered.

"Nope, we are going to stay aboard, just in case we get a break in the weather."

The seas were churning as we 'chummed for company' on our way out of Scituate Harbor on our first day.

That night we had a workable heater so did not need the life preserver qualities of the bourbon and the Beefeater's.

Sunday, October 5 — Finally Under Way

I was up at 0600. The day was bright. The wind was still northeast but had subsided to ten knots, and the seas were rough but less formidable than the day before.

I met John at the seven o'clock mass at Saint Francis, and he said, "What are you going to do?"

"Let's drop my car at Cohasset, and how about taking me back to the marina because I think we're on go."

I brought the Sunday papers back to Milt. We cooked up a big breakfast. Small craft warnings were still up, but we decided, as the weather seemed to be clearing up and as the wind had subsided to eight to ten knots, that maybe we could slip out of the marina and poke around a bit outside. A little taste of the cheese.

Outside the seas were three to four feet and, as we set a course south for the Cape Cod Canal, we had a mixed sea and swell astern and we corkscrewed and churned down the coast. A northeast blow really keeps the sea in a foul mood.

I called Patti on ship-to-shore telephone from Farnham's Rock, en route to the canal, and told her, "We're finally under way."

What a feeling it was!

Milt is good aboard. He told me about the days of yore when he was a merchant marine skipper, then a navy captain, and the more he talked the more confident I was that, if John couldn't make the trip, I had chosen in Milt the right companion.

Now, don't think I lack confidence—I don't—but when things go wrong aboard a yacht it's always reassuring to have an experienced seaman aboard.

There really are lots of guys I could have asked to come with me, but finding a companion who is also a capable seaman and navigator is pretty darn important.

Cape Cod Canal and Point Judith

We were at the Cape Cod Canal at 1157, and I was satisfied that I had come within sixty seconds on my navigation in rough water. Once inside we were in the lee of the canal and it was a millpond for eight miles, and then it was down the Hog Island Channel, past Milt's old school—Massachusetts Maritime Academy—and out to Cleveland's Ledge where the wind picked up like out of nowhere and the seas became heavy, working our starboard quarter. We almost opted for the safety and tranquility of Cuttyhunk Harbor at the end of the Elizabeths, but decided that "no way are we going to get to the Chesapeake this way."

Milt Shaw at the helm with the Cape Cod Canal and the Sandwich Power Station in the background.

So we set a course for Point Judith, forty miles away on the Rhode Island coast.

It was testy at times, especially the last hour, as a thick, shoe-polish-black cloud formation worked over the area over Block Island off our port bow. *Islander* performed well, and the storm cloud did likewise because we slid behind the breakwater at Point Judith at 1730—ninety-three miles from Scituate.

Islander cruised through the Harbor of Refuge, a huge breakwatered area protecting the land from the sea, into the Point Judith Pond which is a delightfully quaint fishing port where the two villages at the head of the pond are called Galilee and Jerusalem.

We used a chart on page 127 of the 1976 edition of the *Boating Almanac* to find our way inside, exploring the docks on the east with its almost 100 commercial fishing boats. But not seeing a

Snug Harbor Marina on the Jerusalem side of delightful Point Judith, our berth the first night out.

suitable marina, we decided to visit the west side and touch base at the Snug Harbor Marina, which we had seen listed in the *Almanac*.

This is where we should have paid closer attention to the chart because, instead of reversing direction and going back to the junction near the harbor entrance, I decided for some unthinkable reason to cast straight across the harbor. I must have thought that I was back in deepwater Scituate Harbor.

I am thankful my Raytheon fathometer was on and working, because when I shocked to see that I had gone quickly from twenty feet of water to two feet, I threw my twin Palmers full astern, poured some horses to them and, with sweat on my brow, backed off what I found out later was a huge mud bank. I shuddered at the thought that the first day out would have been one heck of a time to have disaster number one—perhaps a bent propeller or a fouled-up shaft.

We found Snug Harbor Marina deserted at 1800, so we tied onto the gas dock, washed the boat down, plugged into power, and made ourselves at home. Milt prepared a delicious three-plate supper consisting of chile con carne, bread and chocolate chip cookies. In keeping with this family scene, I washed the dishes.

At 0700 the dockmaster was on hand, and we talked to Marty Jacobson on the *Susan C.* out of Simms Yacht Yard in Scituate, who was cruising to winter storage in Upstate New York. His Egg Harbor, also thirty-seven feet, had also come down the coast that day but was running a half-hour ahead of us. Marty owns the Hull Lobster Company, and I told him I'd be over one of these fine days.

Long Island Sound

We were on our way by 0800, and we began a great cruise up the Long Island Sound—one of the trips I'd always wanted to take.

Our course was past Watch Hill, offshore of beautiful Fishers Island, through the swift current of The Race and then a mid-sound course to New York City.

After a few hours in mid-sound, we opted for a little scenery, so we spent the rest of this delightfully breezy, sun-filled day cruising easily through the slight chop off the Long Island side.

Port Jefferson was a pleasure to see, and we went past places like Oyster Bay, where we promised ourselves that we would return to cruise at leisure on some later trip.

The sun was setting as we approached the funnel which was the end of Long Island Sound and the entryway to the grandeur of New York City.

We saw it first as we passed by Execution Rock which is between New Rochelle and Manhasset Neck. We saw the New York

COMPASS COURSE 180°

Milt intent on his course as we come abeam *The Race* off Fisher's Island, Long Island Sound.

skyline, the Empire State Building, and the twin World Trade Center towers, and I took a half-dozen color slides of the great city's silhouette at sunset.

It was now 1800 when we pulled into the huge Consolidated Shipyard at City Island. It was an immense yard, but everyone but the guard had gone home. So we found an empty slip and tied down for the night. It was a rather sumptuous feeling to be tied down only a few slips from the 125-foot private yacht *Freidreke*, hailing port Monrovia, Liberia, which was built by Feadship in Holland and owned by an American businessman whom, I guess, should remain nameless as I am usually a little suspicious of business people who register their boats out of Monrovian-type ports.

"Sorry, can't get you into the gas dock this morning" was the good-morning report from the dockmaster the following morning. "Too much big traffic—you'll have to wait an hour."

"See you later," we said as we left the austere and commercial surroundings of City Island, New York, not caring if we ever returned. Next time through we shall try to tie down elsewhere—maybe Port Washington on the Long Island side.

I don't like running on half-full tanks, especially in such a super gas-guzzler as *Islander*, but at 0830 with a stiff fifteen-knot breeze picking up we proceeded through grey skies and morning chill under the Throgs Neck Bridge to the famous Hell's Gate Bridge—all the time New York City getting larger and more formidable.

Many people had dispelled horror stories about debris and fierce current at Hell's Gate, but again the angels were with *Islander*, because Hell's Gate was calm and the only debris we saw was on a New York City garbage scow.

New York City

Under Hell's Gate and all New York City opened up in its splendor. Milt was at the helm on the bridge. I was at the chart station to the right of the helm. Both of us were in our fur-lined Maine Guide jackets. Milt had binoculars around his neck. I had my new Konica 16-millimeter camera around my neck. All of our flags and pennants were unfurled and snapping in the stiff breeze: our Scituate Harbor Yacht Club burgee; John's Scituate Harbor Yacht Club Commodore's flag; our Commonwealth of Massachusetts pennant, which Sonny McDonough had given me; our huge red nylon Operation Sail flag, which was lashed high on the starboard antenna; and finally, our proud national ensign off our stern.

It was a glorious moment in life. Coming down New York's East River in our own smart craft, no other traffic on the river, we waved to the people in the bumper-to-bumper traffic of the Franklin Delano Roosevelt Highway. We waved to people in the towering office buildings. We waved up at the United Nations Building. Some people paused from their own busy lives and waved back.

The Peking, London England, is a proud four-master thrust into the midst of the 20th Century in downtown New York City with the East River and the World Trade Towers in the background.

We found a little marina in the heart of the city, right by East 23nd Street, but they pumped Gulf and, as we did not have a proper card, we carried on. But we made a note to remember this place for a future visit to New York City.

We went under the Williamsburg Bridge, the Manhattan Bridge, and finally the eagerly anticipated Brooklyn Bridge. I made some slides of this passage which developed especially well—in particular the one of the Wall Street Towers and the World Trade buildings, framed by the black-grey cables and stanchions of the world's most famous bridge, the Brooklyn Bridge.

Down past the Battery everything was moving—great ferries. tankers, freighters, tugs, our handsome pleasure craft, and we chuckled as even a little seaplane got in the act and took off after a run from behind Governors Island.

The Statue of Liberty was revisited—this time our vantage point being the bridge of the *Islander*, and the old gal looked just fine. I remembered my personal discomfiture of a year or so ago after Patti, Carol and I had climbed the iron stairs into the torch of the great Statue of Liberty. After that climb my legs had ached for a week.

Islander headed due south leaving New York behind, and we cruised under the huge Verrazano Narrows suspension bridge that connects Staten Island with Brooklyn.

A Thrilling Ride to Sandy Hook

We had a decision to make—either pull in behind Sandy Hook for gas or run the thirty-five miles along the New Jersey coast to Manasquan Inlet, a good place to tie up for the night. We stopped our boat, dip-sticked our gas tanks, and opted for Manasquan, as the weather was cloudy and ominous but the sea was no more than *Islander* could easily take, or so it seemed to us at the moment.

Then it hit us. We had crossed past Romer Shoals and started to head south around Sandy Hook. Milt had gone below to put on the generator and make coffee. As we poked farther outside around the Hook, the sea started to build up and up and up. I started to take waves on the bow. My bow was up, then she buried. It was like hitting three-story buildings. It was now decision time again, and I picked a judicious spot between the huge waves, threw my helm to starboard, and set a course that would take me up the channel directly off Sandy Hook. For four miles a mountainous following sea chased me. What a boating thrill! *Islander* again performed like a champion, elevating up one huge wave, riding a crest with a steady keel, then swishing and corkscrewing down the sea-mountain, pulling up nicely, then starting the climb and swish all over again.

Only a fifteen-minute adventure, but what a thrill—more exciting than coming down the ski slopes at Gunstock Mountain. And then it was over—*Islander* had pulled into the lee of Sandy Hook and we had a rainy but calm fifteen-minute cruise to the huge and well-equipped Atlantic Highlands Yacht Basin, where a young and charming lady dockmaster found us dockage when there wasn't any.

To make room for us she had to have Cliff Larson, captain of the beautiful sixty-foot Elcho, *Gladlar*, out of Boston Harbor Marina, pull up tight and we squeezed *Islander* in behind. It was good we did because another small adventure was in the making.

It turned out that the *Gladlar* was a 1931 hull and had been in the Putnam family for many years and that her good captain, Cliff Larson, had been a classmate of Milt Shaw's at Massachusetts Maritime Academy and also knew my brother Bill from Massachusetts Maritime days.

Cliff produced the membership roster of the Academy boys and presented the information that both Milt and Bill were in arrears with their dues and had better do something about it pronto.

There is lots of activity at the Atlantic Highlands in the summer, but very little on rainy and now foggy afternoons, and

Milt and I visited what local bistros there were and then decided to have beef stew aboard and set the alarm for 0500.

The alarm went off on time, but the weather was still foul and small craft warnings were still flying. We cleaned up the boat, took pictures of the old *Alexander Hamilton*, an enormous sidewheeler excursion boat rotting across the harbor. We heard that the Alexander Hamilton Society had bought the hulk and was going to tow her up the Hudson for restoration. Good luck to them. It will be a heroic task.

At 0730 the weather looked like it might clear some, so we decided to crank her up and take a look outside, but here a problem set in because our port engine refused to throw water and the temperature gauge shot up.

I called John, in Scituate, for a bright idea or two and, after I told him I had checked the intake strainers, John suggested that "it might be the impeller or the pump" and that meant a mechanic and a delay. But now enter Captain Larson and his bag of tricks. He had tools for everything and he found our trouble— a belt which was replaced and tightened, and we gave him our grateful thanks.

By 1000 we were again off Sandy Hook. We radioed back to *Gladlar* that the "weather is great—come on out." *Gladlar* reported that the small craft warnings had just come down and he was on his way. It was a short twenty-five-mile run down the Jersey coast, a mile or so offshore to Manasquan Inlet, and here we hit a fog bank so, discretion being the better part of valor, we talked on the radio with *Gladlar* and ran for the inlet with the fog bank chasing us in. We made an A1 entrance between two jetties, but a following sea and a struggling twenty-four-footer in the channel gave us a thrill or two.

A Close Call at Barnegat Shoal

It was a lazy day at beautiful, well-protected Manasquan. We were finishing dinner looking at the scenery, relaxing with the thoughts of our fun—Scituate to Manasquan—and thinking of the days to come.

"It's getting pretty calm out there, Jack," commented Milt. "Look at that moon!"

"Not bad, Milt. Want to make up some time and make a run for it tonight?" I chipped in.

"Why not," said El Milto, and fifteen minutes later we were churning out of the inlet and heading south on a course that should take us well outside of Barnegat Shoal. It was 2215.

We picked off our marks, easily recognizing the tanks and towers as we ran a mile offshore in the moonlight. All went well because it was so clear and the shoreline was silhouetted, but when we came to Seaside State Park we ran out of markers and in the black worked our way towards the ominous Barnegat Shoals.

Milt was at the helm. "Are we out far enough?" he asked.

"Maybe. Keep your eye on the depth finder and edge her to port," I said.

"Plenty of water," answered Milt as he reported thirty feet.

"If we are OK we should spot the lightship any minute." We both strained our eyes looking off our bow for the light.

"Time's up, Milt," I said as I checked my watch against the chart distance. "How's your water 'cause we should be right on."

"No light yet, but I hear something," said Milt. "Sounds like surf, but we're well out."

I stood up on the bridge, listened, and then I saw it flashing in the moonlight—crashing, swirling, frothing surf right off our bow.

"Holy hell, Milt, throw it to port—we're on the shoal," I yelled.

Milt reacted fast. He pulled back power, threw it to port and we both prayed silently as the depth finder recorded two feet under our keel.

"Careful, Milt, careful, inch her out. Watch the depth."

The reading went up—four feet, six feet, ten feet, and we did not breathe an easy breath until it came back up to twenty-five feet. We kept an easterly course and found our mark.

We had been on the very edge of Barnegat Shoal in the black of night, obviously set in by the swells from the east. We had narrowly averted a disaster, because if we had gotten on the shoals we could have badly damaged *Islander* and, if the seas were rough enough, *Islander* might have broken up with the pounding.

My nerves had been tested and, as we got out in deep water, Milt and I had time to reflect on a visitation on Barnegat Shoals in the dead gloom of midnight.

Atlantic City

We had a forty-mile cruise to the waters off Atlantic City, and we stayed well outside of the waters of shoally Beach Haven Inlet and Brigantine Shoals although, at one time off Brigantine, the depthometer momentarily dropped to seven feet, but I wheeled out quickly.

It was about 0300 when we clearly saw the outlines of the great Atlantic City hotels, and the real big fellow we saw outlined must have been Haddon Hall where both Milt and I would be speaking to the New Jersey Realtors Convention in December.

Milt denied that he was either unnerved or tired, but I was both, so I asked Milt to pick us a course for the Atlantic City Boat Basin because a stiff belt of bourbon and a few hours sleep were a must for me.

The entry was tricky at night as the mariner seems to be steering right into the lobby of some hotel, but the key is to keep that great occulting light on the left hand and confidently steam along the seawall and hotels, keeping them to port until the channel takes shape. When we saw a few draggers coming out, one without running lights, we knew we were AOK on course. Then a wide channel opened up on the left, behind the hotels, and we discovered a very welcome, brightly lighted pier. We were the only ones there. We tied down. I took a gigantic drink of bourbon, thanked the good Lord for delivering us safely, and was asleep in thirty seconds.

The decision to sleep for a few hours was a good one, as we awoke refreshed at 0600 and had coffee, doughnuts and chocolate chip cookies on the bridge as again we went back to the sea.

By day we could easily see the shoal waters off Great Egg Harbor Inlet, Carson Inlet, Townsend Inlet and Hereford Inlet, and we reflected back on what Barnegat must have looked like last night at midnight.

Cape May to the Chesapeake to the Sassafras

The cruise to Cape May was three and one-half hours and a joy. We were wearing light sweaters when we pulled into Ernie Visch's marina which is on the left just before you get to the Cape May Canal, the safe little waterway connecting the Atlantic to Delaware Bay.

Ernie was very helpful, and he and his sons, his wife, and the family dog all posed for a picture by the *Islander*. Ernie seemed pleased to have our business, and he commented that most of the big boats seemed to pull to the right into the large Cape Island Marina.

"Where's a good place for us to run to tonight, Ernie—a place where we can safely leave the *Islander* for a few weeks?" we asked.

"Best place I know of is a place on the Sassafras River called the Georgetown Marina. I only saw it once, but it's clean, in perfect condition, and real shipshape. It's the kind of a place where your boat will be safe."

It later was proved that he was so right!

We started up the Cape May Canal at 1030, cruised up the well-marked Delaware Bay—a wide body of water in which there was considerable ship traffic going into Wilmington, Philadelphia and Camden—and by 1600 had arrived at the long-awaited Chesapeake and Delaware Canal, a fifteen-mile-long cut linking the great Delaware Bay with the upper reaches of the Chesapeake Bay.

Ernie Visch had mentioned Schaeffer's Canal House as a convenient spot to stop for gas or dinner, but time was pressing so we moved on and, unfortunately, I threw up more of a wake than I had anticipated and I was very embarrassed at the discomfiture that I caused several boatsmen tied to his dock.

The next hour and a half down the Elk River to the Chesapeake, then hard to port and eight miles up the Sassafras was one of the most glorious periods I ever remember.

The great red sun was setting as we went down the wide and glittering stream—woods on either side, some floating logs and roots. The Canadian geese and other birds seemed to be everywhere. I took some pictures and hoped they would accurately record the scene.

Darkness was just beginning to fall as we worked our way up the Sassafras, and this too was a winding, turning passage, and I thanked the Lord for a good chart because when darkness fell it was ink black.

We inched our way over the last few miles and finally a huge marina area appeared out of the wilderness. The last marina on the right turned out to be our place. Even though no one was there to greet us at 1930, we had radioed ahead, so we knew someone must be expecting us. We picked a convenient empty slip and tied down.

End Phase I

It had been a thirteen-hour run from Atlantic City, and we had cruised eighteen of the past twenty-one hours from Manasquan to Sassafras—a long journey to wind up Phase I of our cruise from

Milt and I said, "rest well" to *Islander* as we left her at the Georgetown Marina on the Sassafras River.

Scituate to Florida. About forty-five hours of boating with about 580 miles covered—a lot of distance, much fun, and great adventure.

Now, to think about returning to Boston.

Laurette Sisk at the marina told us there was a private grassy strip a mile or so away, so I called Bill Kermond in Winchester and asked him if his offer to fly down and pick us up was still open.

He said it was, and eight minutes later Milt and I were asleep.

36 COMPASS COURSE 180°

Friday, October 7, 1976.

Taken Direct From Islander's Log

0800 Awoke in midst of splendor of Georgetown Marina, on the Sassafras River, in Northern Delaware. Weather clear. Slight clouds. Met dockmaster, Laurette Sisk, who logged us aboard at a modest 25 cents a foot per day for the period the *Islander* was to be here. Marina had clean showers, the best equipment, a well-provisioned marine store, and was a joy. Met Guy Wagner, next boat, and we became friends and met his friend Zane, and we all had lunch aboard *Islander*. Milt, suffering from a slight cold, spent most of the A.M. cleaning up the inside of the *Islander*. I scrubbed and scoured the outside, as it was grimy and filthy from the long, long trip south to Chesapeake.

1430 Locked up *Islander*. Gave keys to Laurette and Elsie at the store, drove us to the airstrip where we were to meet Bill Kermond, who was flying down from Boston to pick us up and take us back to the "real world."

1500 Elsie dropped us at nearby Hexton Farms Airfield. It really was something else—a 3200-foot grass strip which is owned by Sam Dupont. I do not know exactly how much room Bill needs for the takeoff, but I hope this is enough because Milt Shaw weighs 180, I go 190, and we must have 40 pounds of baggage, making 410 extra pounds for the plane.

1530 Milt and I are stretched out on the grass strip listening for planes. Visibility rather limited. Maybe 1500 feet, which is a guess. Bill is to come to New Castle, Delaware, take a course of 226 and go for twenty-five miles to this strip which is really not too well marked. There is a big yellow wind sock but, as there is no wind, this is not any help. Rather humorous, in a way, in this day of high-level transportation. We take a boat 500 miles out of Boston, experience some hair-raising experiences, end up at a marina up the end of an eight-mile-long river called Sassafras, leave the boat and then find ourselves alone in the middle of a grassy meadow waiting for a plane that might or might not come and, if it does, might or might not find the field and, if it does find the field, might or might not elect to land.

1545 We are listening for the sound of planes. We hear them but have difficulty seeing them. A minute or so ago Milt said he heard something, but it turned out to be an oil truck. There was a light plane in the sky a minute ago, but we did not see it. There now seems to be a hole in the sky just north of us and maybe Bill will be able to spot it. There's an airliner, maybe at 20,000 feet, and it was visible for a few minutes before we lost it. Canadian geese are everywhere, literally thousands of them—big plump fellows all filled to full girth after feeding in Canada all summer. Now they migrate to the Eastern Shore to spend the winter in the bountiful cornfields. Today they have settled in on a pond by the north end of the runway. I hope Bill does not clobber one when (or if) he comes in for a landing.

1600 No Bill yet. Oh, here comes a small plane right over us. We wave our raincoats as we run out into the middle of the grass strip. We stand on the grass strip right between the cornfields. He sees us, comes around and straight on in without a single thought or a practice run, directly over the Canadian geese area without disturbing a feather. Bill's landing is superlative, and we are aboard and in the air in less than a minute or two.

1705 We lost visibility, and the fog and rain battered our trim single-engine Beachcraft Bonanza as we flew over New York City, but it cleared up over Connecticut. As darkness dropped her curtain Bill picked out Marshfield Airport, eight miles from home. He dropped a wing hard and at

Dr. Bill Kermond, center, in front of his Beachcraft Bonanza on the grass strip at Georgetown with his friend Bob Hoyt, left, and Jack.

1815 came in hard and fast with a fighter-pilot landing. John Reardon was there waiting for us, and this thrilling leg of our journey to Florida on the *Islander* had come to an end.

PHASE II

SASSAFRAS RIVER TO MOREHEAD CITY, NORTH CAROLINA

Back in Massachusetts it was difficult keeping my mind entirely on work because I kept thinking about the next leg of our journey south which would take *Islander* out of the Sassafras, down the Chesapeake and as far below Norfolk as possible. I picked out Elizabeth City and Belhaven, North Carolina as the two possible destinations before leaving *Islander* at the end of Phase II.

Now to find a crew! I kept telling John Reardon about the sensational time we had running *Islander* from Scituate to the Sassafras, and he kept agreeing that he sure wished he had been aboard. I let it drop there. And then, one night, I got an excited call from John with the news that Mary was feeling pretty well now and that he had gotten clearance to join me on Phase II. I certainly was very happy about this. Now the trick was to set a departure date and figure out how we were going to get to the Georgetown Marina, a quiet beautiful place, but off any beaten path and somewhat difficult to reach.

I called my brother-in-law, Ray Maher, at Baltimore and asked him if he could provide some sort of transportation if John and I were to fly into Friendship Airport on Thursday morning, October 28th at about 8:15 A.M. on the first Allegheny flight out of Boston.

40 COMPASS COURSE 180°

Islander's crew for Phase II were cold but enthused as they make ready to go down the Sassafras to the Chesapeake. L. to r, Ray Maher; Richard McClung, the driver; John Reardon and Jack. Richard left us here.

Being the retail advertising manager of the *Baltimore Sun*, I figured, was enough of a qualifying opener for Ray to be asked to help us work out this logistical problem.

"As a matter of fact," said Ray on the phone, "I'll not only work out your transportation problem but I'll come with you."

"Hey! Great!" I answered, and the crew was arranged and the trip was planned.

Return to the Islander

So, on the morning of Thursday, October 28, 1976, just twenty days after we had ended Phase I, we were ready to go again. John and I left Boston on an 0700 Allegheny flight to Friendship Airport in Baltimore. Ray and his young friend, Richard, met us at the plane, and by 1030 we had arrived aboard *Islander*, having

COMPASS COURSE 180° 41

Ray Maher is at the helm of *Islander* as Jack points to the huge Bay Bridge which leapfrogs the Chesapeake at Annapolis.

provisioned it with all sorts of delicacies such as canned sardines, Franco American spaghetti, lots of fresh, raw oysters, and a new supply of good Miller's High Life.

The weather was cold, nipping raw cold, twenty-nine degrees cold, windblown cold, numb hands on aluminum cold, red-spotted cheeks cold, as we moved down the Sassafras to the Chesapeake. The scenery was enchanting—the weather, bone chilling. The river wound and turned and we picked our channel with care. It was good we did because the numbering system on the river was not completely in concurrence with that on the chart.

We picked up a current on the Chesapeake, and *Islander* really started to open up. We left Baltimore to starboard, cruised under the two mammoth spans of the Chesapeake Bay Bridge, of heroic proportions, where we all posed for pictures with the bridge in the background.

The port of Annapolis was off to the right, and the port of Saint Michaels was tucked away on the left bank—the Eastern Shore. I had read about Saint Michaels in *National Geographic* and made a mental note that on some day on some other trip I would visit it, but today our destination was the Solomons, daylight permitting. We definitely needed daylight because we had heard tales that the entry channel was a challenging one.

Tilghman Island

Ray, John and I had a conference on the bridge about 1600 as we came abeam of Poplar Island. I had calculated it would be a good strong two hours to the Solomons, so we checked our chart and found the nearest port was Tilghman Island.

"Hey, I've been there and it's great," said Ray. "We took a *Sun* advertising group there for fishing a couple of times and I'd say 'Let's go there.'"

So we swung the helm of *Islander* to port and made a course to Tilghman Island.

It was a cautious entry because the channel was narrow, but when we got inside the jetty a whole world opened up for us.

Tilghman is an oyster port. Some of the local folks later told us it is the capital of the oyster world, and the long narrow finger of a harbor—actually Knapps Narrows, which bisects the island— teems with those forty-two-foot narrow-beamed oyster boats called "Bug eyes." These busy little single-screw craft are manned by a crew of two—a captain and a mate—and they hand tong the oysters from the shallow surrounding waters. Hand tonging seems like really hard work and the watermen we talked to are weathered and hard but shrewd and content with their work. One old fellow admitted to being in his eighties, insisting that "I never miss a day on the bay."

We found a friendly greeting at "Mac" McKendricks's Esso dock, just before the bridge, and before the night was over Mac had

Oyster Boats (Bug eyes) off-load their oyster treasure at Tilghman's Island.

joined us aboard to tell us of his own new adventure—the Esso dock, store and marina that he had purchased less than a year before.

"I had spent twenty years as an engineer for Scott paper, then General Electric," he told us, "and the pressure was building all the time. Job insecurity really is something that gets to a guy. So I looked around for something I could run myself, found this little place advertised for sale in the *Baltimore Sun*, quit my job, sold my $75,000 house, and here we are—a family working long hours, but happy."

"How do you get along with the Tilghman Islanders?" asked Ray, because he knew them to be an old-line, well-entrenched, close-knit society.

"I'm playing it easy. They do business with me, I respect them, and little by little we are sort of getting accepted. As a matter of fact, awhile back we were invited over to the home of one of the watermen and we really got on fine, at least I hope we did," he said.

Mac suggested we try the nearby Bridge Restaurant for dinner. "It's right over on the other side of the inlet, and they serve all of the raw oysters you can eat for a dollar—then you have dinner."

I have never had so many oysters in all my life. I must have had twenty-five of them—big, fat, juicy ones, and such a contrast to raw oysters at any good hotel restaurant where a half-dozen raw oysters would cost $3.50 at least.

For dinner, naturally we stayed with the menu of the island and had fried oysters.

With stomachs full and perhaps overfilled, we decided to take the mile-long walk up the now-deserted main street of the island to Captain Levin Harrison's Chesapeake House for a relaxing scotch.

The Chesapeake House was a rather large, rambling wooden structure of a pre-turn-of-the-century vintage, and the host Captain Harrison was right on hand to greet us.

White haired, well-dressed, courtly and very pleasant, he was glad to see Ray Maher again.

"Been a long time since you were out fishing with us," he said. "You remember my son Buddy," and we all shook hands with Buddy who was perhaps forty and a fishing boat captain. We enjoyed the hospitality of the old captain and when it came time to depart, we readily accepted his offer to drive us back to *Islander*. His shiny new Cadillac sedan was in sharp contrast to everything else we had seen on Tilghman Island.

Chesapeake Bay

It was black dark at 0600 when we made ready to cast off and say "good-bye" to Tilghman harbor. We had breakfasted, checked out our engines and now only waited for the first crack of light so that we could pick our way out of the narrow little channel.

It seemed that the Tilghman Island oyster fleet also had the same idea of getting off to an early start because what seemed like an army of long, thin trim "Bug eyes" started revving up their engines, switching on their red and green running lights, and pulling out into an ant-like procession towards the waters of the Chesapeake Bay.

It was an inspiring sight, and we took our opportunity for an early start and squeezed into this line of march setting our course through the darkness of predawn on the stern light of the vessel in front of us, and away we went down the channel, past the piers and docks, past the jetty and down the ribbon ditch to deep water.

Out in the Chesapeake it was again cold, but we stayed on the bridge for all of the extra visibility that we could get as we set course for a green flasher in the ship channel. As we moved southwesterly, we could easily make out the light on fifty-four-foot high Sharps Island light, a place for another future trip because behind it is the Choptank River and the waters leading to the other interesting Eastern Shore ports like Oxford and Cambridge.

We came down on the entrance to the Patuxent River at thirteen knots out of the darkness and, as morning broke upon us, we were well upon our way to the waters off the Solomons which had been our destination the night before. When we studied on the charts the rather intricate channel system opening from the mouth of the Patuxent into the harbor of the Solomons, we figured it had been a wise choice to tie up at Tilghman rather than attempt to reach the Solomons in the dark.

Ray and John on the bridge as *Islander* enters Norfolk Harbor.

We swept into a current and our speed moved up to 15.5 knots, our fastest ever, as we glided past Smith Island, Tangiers, the mouth of the Potomac which suggested another day and another trip—one which would take the *Islander* up to the capital of the nation. Then we passed the mouth of the Rappahannock, so often appearing in the stories of the battles of the Civil War.

Ominous sounding Wolfe Trap was on our starboard hand as we cruised in the now warmer sunlight of an early afternoon on a thrilling October day—wind crisp, slight chop, bright dancing waters. We left the entry of the York River behind, and by 1530 we were on a course to Thimble Shoals and Hampton Roads.

Liner *United States* at rest in Norfolk.

Naval Operations Base

What an exciting moment it was for us to enter this great bastion of United States Navy strength and power, and my mind flashed back to thoughts of how busy it was in the port thirty-three years ago when this was the supply base for much of what happened on D Day at Omaha Beach. Back in those days I was swab jockey, U.S. Navy style, attached to Landing Ship Medium 125 at the Little Creek Amphibious Base just out of Norfolk. Now, years later, I was entering the waters of my previous naval duty at the helm of *Islander*, a rather pleasant transition of the years.

Busy little tug and Coast Guard Cutter bustling at work in active Norfolk.

We cruised past the old Naval Operations Base, a place I had known well because it was there I had spent six months of my life in a bed at Ward 26D recovering from the orthopedic surgery which saved my right leg from amputation—a job well-done by a navy commander from Wisconsin named Dr. Jim Nellen.

When the long, graceful hull of the *United States* hove into view, we had an unexpected experience because she, the all-time largest passenger liner in the United States, built in the ways of the nearby Newport News Shipyard, was now laid up in a berth at the Naval Operating Base. And she was heading, according to rumor, for a new life as a floating tourist hotel in Boston Harbor. We got some fine photographs of her.

The warships, some obviously in service, others in various stages of repose, were in ample abundance as we drew closer and closer to Norfolk. Carriers, cruisers, destroyers, supply ships—they were all there—rather like big Newfoundland dogs lying by the fireplace dozing and waiting for something to happen.

COMPASS COURSE 180°

Delayed by the Railroad

We had been advised by Jim Tweedy, our friend from Scituate, to stopover at the Holiday Harbor Marina on the Portsmouth side of the junction of the east and the south branches of the Elizabeth River as it winds its way between Port Norfolk and Portsmouth on the west and Norfolk on the east.

It really was a well-stocked marina—plenty of everything except the one thing that they had advertised in the *Boating Almanac*—charts of the Intracoastal Waterway. So, after signing up for a slip for the night and finding that they did not have the charts that I needed, I showed my indignation by telling them "au revoir" and "please let someone else have my slip as we are going to steam to Great Bridge and get both a berth for the night as well as our charts" which we had been informed they had in abundance.

Time was with us as it was only 1645, and ten miles to the Atlantic Yacht Basin at Great Bridge was not much we thought, but we had a lot to learn. Downstream, a mile or two, after seeing 100 or more naval ships—some active, some tired and asleep, and some just rafted together—subs, destroyers, LSD's, supply ships, DE's, sub chasers, you name it, including the old Portsmouth Lightship, red-painted and entangled in a Disney-world-type setting as a tourist visitation altar, a touch of the romantic sea history of yesteryear—we came to a bridge. The bridge! It was a railroad bridge and it was down and, as down as the bridge was, so was the sun—ebbing. Would not the dear old black hulk of iron open for boat passage? No, it would not. Fifteen minutes, twenty, then a half-hour, as we lay off, holding position, now and then hooting our horn, now circling, and then doing a figure eight. Keep cool—watch the sun go down—after all, running in a strange canal to Great Bridge is a joy forever.

A long toot—a train toot—and we found out why the bridge would not open and let us through. First came a sixty-car train

Portsmouth Lightship now a dockside museum.

from the west—coal cars, grain cars, hopper cars, flat cars, oil cars. We in New England hardly ever see such a train.

Now, we felt, the bridge would open and allow us to capture the last few minutes of the daylight, but it did not. Another toot—another train—this one coming from the east, probably from the docks at Lambert Point above Norfolk by Hampton Roads— and double-tiered with Ford pickup trucks, all colors. I have never seen so many Ford pickup trucks. I took pictures as the trucks silhouetted between the huge stanchions of the bridge. Time

We waited and waited for the railroad bridge to open and the long train of little trucks seemed endless.

passed and it was after 1830 when we finally passed under the bridge. It was getting dark very quickly.

Over John's objections, I really threw the power to dear old *Islander*. The waterway speed limit was six knots. I was running against nighttime and we plowed on at twelve knots spilling waves of wash on the broad banks and then, to keep our recent record intact, we turned a bend in the river to come upon the Gilmerton, Norfolk and Western Railroad bridge where again we watched a suitable length freight train do its thing, hauling something or another to Lambert Point.

Great Bridge Lock

By now we had lost all pretense of defeating darkness, so we just chugged on deciding to make the best of a questionable situation. We overtook a long barge tow on the bend between New Mill Creek and Sykes Creek, squeezing by in the narrow channel, getting a wave from the captain of the monster tug *Crochet* which flew the house flag of the Norfolk Dredging Company. Then we poured it on as we made a two-mile "me and my arrow" shot towards the blazing white lights of the 600-foot Great Bridge lock.

This was my first experience in a lock and, believe me, it was an adventure of the first magnitude to be snugged into this huge 600-by 75-foot lock, all alone, the only boat, and watch as the gates closed on us. We wondered what would happen. Would we go up, or would we go down?

It was now 1930, dark as can be, but our destination, the Atlantic Yacht Basin, Great Bridge, Virginia was only a half-mile the other side of the lock and the long pier for the transient yachts paralleled the waterway, so we felt once out of the lock we would have an easy enough time of it.

Ray Maher hollered to me from up on the grassy ridge of the lock, "Hey, Jack, the lock is opening again." I looked back. Progress had stopped. The lock tender had spotted the *Crochet* and her long line of dredging barges, their red and green running lights visible far up the ditch, and had decided to wait for the oncoming vessel.

There went our time schedule, or at least what was left of it, because before the huge *Crochet* had settled in astern of *Islander* and had gotten her long tow of barge chickens doubled up in tandem position, the lock was full to the bulging waistband with big tugs, little pusher tugs and barges, all sorts of barges, huge pipe-carrying barges, crane barges, crew barges and just plain junk barges.

The skipper of the *Crochet* told us about how the *Crochet* had been "up to Winthrop, Massachusetts on a sewerage dredging job last winter and cold! How do you people take that cold?"

Stashing away a barge tow in a 600-by 75-foot lock is no mean job. The stress on the eight-inch hawsers looped over the bollards on the rim of the lock created an uncomfortable wrenching of the tensil strength of the manila fibre as one barge moved, making a second barge react and, in turn, bring an almost unbelievable force on the stretched hawsers.

"Any chance that these lines might not hold?" I asked the captain of the *Crochet* as I watched my little *Islander* scrunched up into a corner of the lock as these Goliaths indian-wrestled for position just off her stern.

"No, they ought to hold," said the captain of the *Crochet*. He seemed to absorb some of my anxiety because after my timidly-stated question he called for two more great hawsers to be put into play, thus securing more fastly the position of his chickens.

Now at 2130, five hours after we had left the Holiday Marina, ten miles upstream, we were out of the lock and tying up at the well-equipped Atlantic Yacht Basin. It had been an interesting adventure in boating yet a real long time to cover ten miles—fifteen and one-half hours aboard the *Islander,* but the great weather and new horizons and adventure made it all more than worthwhile.

The next morning was also just fine, and we all had slept well aboard the *Islander* at dockside. The well-equipped marine store had everything we needed in charts. This yard, looping out back into a broad marine area, accommodated some large yachts. Their marine repair facilities were as good as I had seen, and there must have been six or seven huge storage sheds, some of them wet storage inside and, from what I learned, their monthly rates for storage were definitely in line and competitive. Several of the yacht owners we met make the Florida run in two stages—southward to Great Bridge, then leave the yacht for a few weeks in wet storage, then Great Bridge to southern Florida—an interesting idea for some future day inasmuch as Great Bridge is approximately the mid-mile mark between Scituate and Fort Lauderdale.

The Intracoastal Waterway

The morning of Saturday, October 23rd, was a thoroughly delightful day—crisp, in the fifties, sunny, clear, with promises of warmer weather to come as the day progressed. What a day to begin our cruise down the officially designated waters of the Intracoastal Waterway.

Our first leg was an eight-mile run down the long ditch that was the Albemarle-Chesapeake Canal—a 100-foot wide man-dredged waterway connecting the south branch of the Elizabeth River, which had taken us much of the way through Norfolk, with the North Landing River.

Mist was on the canal. Swamp maple and oak trees were turning bright red. The pine was everywhere. The great lowlands of the sparsely inhabited surrounding areas were truly both mysterious yet lovely. It was different from any other waters we had cruised. Man had done a wonderous thing in connecting by canal ditch the abundant waters, rivers, creeks and sounds of our Atlantic Coastal regions.

From North Landing the river wound, bent and twisted in an ever southerly course over a narrow, protected 100-foot wide area for another ten miles—an hour at our reduced cruising speed. Here the beauty really became increasingly intense. The swamp meadows opened up. We came upon solitary fishermen in little aluminum-hulled outboards, and we throttled back to almost idle so as not to cause a wake. These men rarely acknowledged our courtesy but just kept fishing remembering, perhaps, other cruisers who had not shown as much courtesy.

We saw all kinds of hulks of rotting and rusted barges in some of the offshoot creeks, and we wondered if these were the visible

Views were spectacular on the Albemarle-Chesapeake Canal.

remains of the millions of tons of barge traffic that plied the Intracoastal during the days of World War II when the German U-Boat menace stabbed the U.S. East Coast and sent traffic scrambling for protected waters whenever possible.

These canals and little rivers are not too deep, maybe averaging eight to ten feet in the dead center, so they are perfect for those great flat-bottomed barges which are either pushed or towed by tugs.

We cruised past Pungo Ferry, a small dock, a few houses, a swing bridge, a port for a fleet of small fishing boats, all snugly tied to a long dock. We made mental note of this as a possible refuge during some other trip.

Now the river opened up and we left Virginia to cross into North Carolina—another adventurous moment, and John pushed hard on the horn button to cheer in the great event—our entry into our eighth state since leaving Scituate. Rhode Island, Connecticut, New York, New Jersey, Delaware, Maryland, Virginia and now North Carolina. Such fun!

The next twenty miles were among the most pleasant of the cruise. John and Ray alternately ran the boat, one at the helm, the other on charts, while we cruised the now broad waters of the North Landing into Currituck Sound. The water was glass. It had warmed into the sixties, and as *Islander* cruised on down the well-marked channel past islands of pine, shores of waving swamp grass, isolated little areas of vacation cottages, through many coveys of ducks and birds, I happily sipped coffee and wrote paragraph after paragraph in the log of the *Islander*. It really was amusing, to me at least, to have weeks of the actual journey behind us and to be writing the description of our trip down the East River of New York, as *Islander* now cut the tight North Carolina passage between Long Point and Piney Island.

Finally our natural waterway ended and we entered a beeline five-mile canal called the North Carolina Cut which connects the North River with the South. There was nothing so sensationally different about the North Carolina Cut because the natural beauty continued to be dramatic. Wild, swampy regions, old gnarled trees rotting at the rootline, their root systems exposed from the evergoing wakes of boats washing against the banks, and then dying and toppling into the shallow waters.

Civilization during these hours meant to us any collection of houses, docks, a gas pump or people. Now we had found one—Coinjock, North Carolina, in the Cut is fifty miles south of where the Elizabeth River bisects Norfolk, the site of a fine marina, restaurant and gas dock, and is indeed another place to mentally head for on another day, another journey.

Albemarle Sound

The North River at first twisted and turned in the beginning of the fifteen-mile run to Albemarle Sound and then it grew wider and wider, to almost three miles wide at one point, to surrounding lowlands now flashing back their brownish-green welcome in the bright morning sun.

We had heard considerable stories about Albemarle Sound, an open body of water perhaps fifteen miles across and perhaps three times that distance wide. Jim Tweedy warned that "when it blows on Albemarle Sound, make ready for a rough passage because the average depth is only fifteen to eighteen feet and the waves really build up."

Buddy Harrison had told us when we visited Chesapeake House on Tilghman Island that "Albemarle Sound can be one mean piece of water."

Allen Fisher, Jr., in his book *America's Inland Waterway* had quoted experienced boatsmen as referring to Albemarle Sound as "the roughest, most treacherous body of water in the entire Atlantic Intracoastal route where the seas often become unpredictable and the waves take on a steepness not always warranted by the strength of the wind."

Fisher had traversed Albemarle in a ten-knot breeze and had encountered a slight chop. We were cruising in a near-flat calm and, after all, we were aboard *Islander*, a yacht built and designed for the rough Atlantic but we still, after the many cautions, approached Albemarle Sound with reverent respect. I got a shot of the big entry marker "A.S." in the channel, but for the next hour and a quarter it was flat, flat calm and we left the much-heralded sound and moved into the three-mile-wide Alligator River, another area where other boatsmen say the water can get testy when the wind is from the wrong quarter. The Alligator is cypress swamp country and the uninhabited scenery continued.

Finally the long, straight run through the twenty-five miles of the Alligator River and Pungo River Canal, around the bend into the Pungo, and then the short seven-mile run up broad waters into Belhaven where we found dockage just inside of the wood-planked jetty at the River Forest Marina, another memorable place on the Intracoastal Waterway.

The River Forest Marina

It had been a good day on the Intracoastal, and *Islander* had left 100 miles of water off her stern, but now at 1730 the darkness was fast falling and dock space was more than welcome.

"Throw me your lines and pull up to the pump, plenty of room, keep 'er comin'," were the first words we heard from a fascinating character named Paul who seemed to be the dockmaster at River Forest.

When we thanked Paul, he immediately started to tell us a series of unrelated incidents about how long he had faithfully served the cruising public; about how well he had secured the lines for these tired cruising yachtsmen; about how well he had watched over their craft as they went ashore to eat at the River Forest Manor; about how many close and true friends he had on the waterway; about how lucky we had been to have crossed Albemarle on a calm day, "Better mark the date in your log book as it may never happen again"; about how convinced he is that "most boats will take more punishment than their skippers can"; and finally about how poorly most yachtsmen, especially sailboaters, appreciated the services of the dockmaster.

"Yes sah, those sailboaters are the worst; do all sorts of things and hardly never get a thank-you from anyone," continued Paul.

I thanked Paul again for his kindness, went aboard *Islander*, slipped a couple of green ones off the roll and returned to the dock where I gave Paul the hand of understanding, the international hand of friendship.

"I knew I was going to like you fellas just the minute you threw me your lines. It really is great to have someone 'preciate what you do for them. Pull down the side of the dock, get in behind the big mud bank, and work over to that small dock over there, not too much water, five feet maybe, and tie down behind that houseboat," directed Paul, the warm breath of new-found friendship exploding around him. "Anything else you want—ice, beer, anything—just call Paul. I'll take care of it."

The best advice the old-timer gave us was to eat at the River Forest Manor. The proprietor and host is Axson Smith who maintains a claim to earlier hotel training at the Drake and the Palmer House in Chicago. Now, I have stayed at the Palmer House on a few occasions, and it is a good enough hostelry, but the Drake! That is indeed something worth noting on one's official resume! The Drake is among America's finest. I have stayed there 100 or more nights. Their lakefront rooms from the sixth floor up are among the finest in the country, and their Cape Cod Room is a delight for the seafood gourmet.

Wherever Axson Smith got most of his experience, be it at the Drake, the Palmer House, or at the River Forest Manor, he learned well because the smorgasbord buffet table at this handsome old Victorian manor house is one of the most enjoyable I have tasted.

The setting, too, is noteworthy. The old place was built back in 1899 by a man named John Aaron Wilkinson, who owned a lumber company and was also vice president of the Norfolk and Southern Railroad. Italian craftsmen had carved ornate ceilings, wood-carvers had created great oak mantels—all different—for the eleven mammoth fireplaces. Heavy paneling was everywhere.

Axson told us the nobility of stage, screen, radio, TV, high opera, finance, affluence, high society and even Twiggy, had been his guests. Now *Islander* too—Ray, John and Jack—may have room at the foot of this altar.

After dinner, Paul was again on hand to accept compliments for the fine meal at his boss's restaurant that he had so willingly recommended; and to give us a brochure telling us, among other things, that we were 833 boating miles from Boston and 801 boating miles to Fort Lauderdale, our possible destination.

"Kin I getcha anything else?" asked Paul.

"How about bringing a few cases of beer down to the boat," suggested John because the sun gets over the yardarm pretty early on the Intracoastal.

In a flash Paul was back with the beer. In a flash John paid the $9.60 a case for the beer. Then, in another flash, he cemented our ongoing, never-to-be-taken-lightly friendship with Paul who thanked us profusely and was off to the other dock, where he engaged another yachtsman with stories proving without a doubt that sailboaters were really a pretty cheap crowd and could he stiffen up a few lines, or get some ice, or do somethin'!

This is the kind of a chuckle that a cruising yachtsman really enjoys as the day winds down and the thoughts turn to tomorrow and the adventures that will lie ahead.

John and Ray topped off a "good-night" scotch as they read the chart for tomorrow's voyage.

I checked our lines and passed an evening hour with a group of adventurous souls who were tied down just forward of us in their forty-foot much-used houseboat.

"We are out of Quincy, Massachusetts," said the skipper. "There are six of us aboard—my wife and I and another couple, plus a couple of youngsters.

"We sold our auto body repair business in Abington, Massachusetts, right near your office, packed all of our auto body repair equipment in the hold of the houseboat, and we are now heading for Tampa where we will start a new life in the sun," beamed the enthusiastic, stocky skipper who appeared to be in his late thirties.

As much of an adventure as this trip was for us, how much more so it must be for this courageous group. Here they were traversing the waters between Massachusetts and Florida, not only in a craft much less seaworthy than *Islander*, but also they were in the process of uprooting a whole life's work, packing the tools of their trade in the hold of their houseboat and pioneering off to a new state, a new business adventure, an entirely new life.

I thoroughly admired their courageous approach and determination of purpose.

Last Day, Phase II

The alarm clock on *Islander* clanged at 0500. It was black, pitch black, as we made our way from the dock through the pine grove to the Manor House to clean up for the day ahead. It was again worth a chuckle to see Paul, still on duty, asking what he could do to make life more pleasant for us waterway transients.

By 0600, still inky black, we had uncovered our bridge, kicked over our engines and, as we cast off our lines and moved softly and quietly from the dock, we all felt a certain thrill.

We were the only boat moving in the marina. The whole world was asleep and as we passed around the wooden bulkhead and into the channel, cruising at a ghostly pace, it felt like we were off to discover something never discovered before.

As we had to start making arrangements for us all to get back to work, we charted a course for Morehead City, North Carolina, a port that Captain Ray of the *Summerwind*, whom we had met on the dock the previous evening, had recommended.

"The Morehead City Yacht Basin is on a canal to the right, just before you go under the big Morehead City-Beaufort Bridge," he said. "Ask for James, the dockmaster. He's black, an old-timer, and he's been running that dock for as long as I can remember. Tell him I said to take good care of you."

Morehead City was only sixty miles down the waterway, so it would be a nice, easy cruise at ten to twelve knots, and our ETA was sometime shortly after noon.

I was at the helm, John was at the chart station, and Ray was in the galley. He had turned on our reliable Onan generator and was heating up the last of Anne Jones' beef stew, now a veteran member of our provision larder—the good old beef stew and the recently devoured chile con carne had served us well and when, and if, this voyage gets completed I vowed, our victory celebration will be the staples of our waterway menu—beef stew, chile con carne, chocolate chip cookies and Miller's beer.

We ate our wonderful breakfast, the stew plus chocolate chip cookies, as the light of the new day exploded above. Such a sight—the bursts of reds and oranges fighting their fiery way through the black grey!

We cruised quietly, all alone on the wide and scenic Pungo River, while this miracle of nature evolved around us. I am sure I will never, ever forget this greatest of all beef stew breakfasts.

Relaxing as this was, we had our time schedule to meet because we had told Bill Kermond that we would call him on ship-to-shore promptly at 1100 because he had told us that "if the flying weather is OK, I'll buzz down from Boston and pick you lads up at Beaufort early Sunday."

No way could we rouse the marine operator as we made a test call from the Pungo, but 1100 hours was a long way down the line and we were sure communication would improve.

We had to momentarily interrupt our radio work off Wade's Point, as we had to play dodger with an oncoming pusher-type tug which was all over the channel, not being able to make up his mind which way he wanted to go.

Waterway Etiquette

It was on the Goose Creek Canal just below the Hobucken Bridge, an hour or so later, when we noticed that we were being overtaken by one of the boats out of the River Forest Marina. She was coming fast in the canal, and when I put the glasses on her I recognized her as our friend *Summerwind*, the handsome 44-foot Hatteras.

We were now about to get one of our boat lessons on waterway etiquette. *Summerwind* emitted three short blasts on her horn signalling to us that she was overtaking and ready to pass.

This time we had learned how to act because, in a similar situation the day before, *Charger* out of Providence, another fast Hatteras, had come on us in a narrow canal with a driving force of speed. *Charger* had sounded her horn but we had continued our ten-knot speed. *Charger* hesitated for a moment, then poured it to her and the wash in the narrow, shallow canal was horrendous. I have some fine pictures of *Charger* coming on, but it was an uncomfortable minute or two as we hung on to our coffee cups on the bridge.

Later that same evening at River Forest Manor, the skipper of *Charger*—a cocky, arrogant and uncouth little character—told John and me that "it was too bad if I threw you a wake back there, but on the waterway when an overtaking yacht sounds her horn, pull back your speed and flatten out. Otherwise I just throw the power to her and to hell with you."

Now we had learned, and we were ready. When *Summerwind* tooted, we pulled back power and she did likewise. Ray, on the bridge of *Summerwind*, indicated that we should pull back even more, and we did, flattening out at two or three knots and completely killing our wake. Then *Summerwind*, at low idle, cruised by us without a ripple and, as soon as she was far enough ahead of us, Ray pushed his throttles ahead and *Summerwind* flew out into the dizzily bright sun-drenched waters of wide Bay River.

Every hour we learned something new on this splendid Intracoastal Waterway.

Morehead City

By 1000 we had turned into the beautiful Neuse River, but we were still unable to raise the marine operator, so we thought that perhaps we should change course and pull into nearby Oriental, a few miles off to starboard, and try to call Bill at a pay station. But then we decided against losing a valuable hour and proceeded.

The view continued to be breathtaking as we cruised the Neuse. John and Ray were alternately at the controls as I enjoyed sipping cup after cup of coffee and writing pages after pages in the "Log of the *Islander*."

The Neuse continued to New Bern, but we swung our helm to port and bent our way into the twenty-mile-long Adams Creek Canal—a ribbon that would bring us to our destination, Morehead City.

It was a minute or two before 1100 when I switched on the marine radio and spoke our call letters into the microphone. "Marine operator, marine operator, this is the Yacht *Islander*, Whiskey Yankee Zebra 3350, do you read me?"

How surprised we all were when a voice came back, "*Islander*, this is marine operator. I read you loud and clear."

I was talking to my sister Carol in Winchester, Massachusetts, seconds later, but she reported that conditions in Boston were "ice" and that Bill had opted "not to fly today." So with our private plane departure now cancelled, we relaxed on the bridge, uncorked a cool Miller's, and set about the business of getting to Morehead City.

When we got out of the canal we found the wide waters before Morehead City alive with pleasure boats, all fishing. There was lots of activity as the area was just inside Cape Lookout and Beaufort Inlet and the fish coming in from the Atlantic were abundant.

In due time we were hailing James Heston who, true to Ray's promise, was handling yacht traffic at the Morehead City Yacht Basin.

"Sure I know the *Summerwind*," he said as he made our lines fast to the gas dock. "Don't you worry. Your boat will be safe here. I'll take care of you."

James was true to his word because after I had backed her down into one of the ample slips, James came aboard and made all sorts of lines fast to pilings and dock.

Dockmaster James Heston was there to greet us at the Morehead City Marina.

"We are going to leave her here for about three weeks, James. Are you sure she'll ride all right?" asked John.

This hit an exposed nerve with James because he now told us about his twenty-five years at this dock and about how he'd tied down huge yachts in the wild of a hurricane. John was sorry he had asked the question.

We knew this was the place and James Heston was the man.

The trip back to Boston was accomplished, but not with any simple ease. We found a cab driver who, for $30, would take us to the airport at New Bern, but by the time we got there we had missed the plane. So we rented an Avis and set out for Washington, D.C., 300 miles upstream.

It was one of those mini-compact jobs which Ray and John drove. I was wedged in the back seat with the luggage, and the boys followed the philosophy that "now that we got him in there, let's let him stay." So I alternately sat and slept in an amazingly comfortable corkscrew position.

At Washington, we again missed the plane, so John and I checked in at Ho Jo's and Ray drove off to Baltimore.

John and I arrived back in Boston the next morning happy with the thrill of piloting *Islander* to the halfway mark in our eventful cruise.

How soon would the cruise continue? Time would tell.

PHASE III

MOREHEAD CITY TO SWANSBORO

John and I were busy at home, and we had little time to think about *Islander*. We were winding up the busiest and best season with our real estate business, and the plan for moving *Islander* farther south was "somewhere down the line but not right this minute."

We did not even have time to discuss who would be in the crew or what our possible destination would be. But a few weeks passed and as we caught up with the work that had piled up as a result of our Sassafras-Morehead City leg, we started to take a few side glances at the desk calendar and mentally juggled appointments around so as to free up five or six days.

The charts indicated that Jacksonville, Florida was about 475 miles south of Morehead City, and this figured about four days if everything clicked, or five days at a more relaxed pace.

So—that was it—Jacksonville, Florida next!

John, however, felt that two of us out of the office together at this particular time was not really prudent, so I called Milt and said, "Milt, how do you feel about another run on *Islander*? Maybe four or five days from Morehead City to Jacksonville?"

Milt is the fastest man with an appointment calendar I have ever known, and in a flash of time we settled on Wednesday, in mid-November, a day that we both were to leave Houston for Boston following the national meetings.

Milt Shaw in nautical mood as we make ready to depart from Morehead City.

"Great," he answered. "I'm on go! How about flying Houston/Atlanta/New Bern, gassing up and setting her rolling?"

And that's just what happened. By late afternoon on the appointed Wednesday we were telling James Heston what an able job he had done taking care of the boat and were about ready to throw our dock lines for a twenty-two-mile run down to Swansboro, which we hoped to reach before dark.

"I don't advise that," warned James. "It's a tight channel and no way are you going to make Swansboro before dark. You just stay here and leave early in the morning."

So we visited Morehead City that evening—a fine little port— busy and bustling with commercial fishermen and all sorts of sporty fishing party boats. Picturesque and salty—a big, wide main street and a good waterfront street.

Tony and The Sanitary Seafood Restaurant

James had recommended a great restaurant for dinner—The Sanitary Seafood Restaurant—and we figured any restaurant with a name like that just had to be good, and we later admitted that it was the perfect choice.

Not only was it clean and the clam chowder and broiled fish sensational, but we also got a chance for a talk with Tony Seaman, the owner.

"Sure liked your restaurant," Milt told Tony as we were about to leave. "Maybe you could tell me about all those pictures that you have on the wall," asked Milt as he pointed to the walls of photos depicting Tony with all sorts of people.

This was just like someone saying to a sailor back from a long voyage, "How'd you like to meet a beautiful young lady, sailor?"

Tony lunged—and I mean lunged—at the opportunity to tell us about his photo gallery, and Milt and I had a thoroughly delightful time hearing about how the greats and near-greats of the waterway think Tony Seaman is just about Number One in their book. Governors, actors, actresses, millionaires, railroad tycoons, great athletes, senators—they all were in complete agreement on one issue: Tony, their confidant, their pal!

I told Tony that I would send him an Honorary Degree in the Conway College of Real Estate Knowledge suitable for framing, of course, and on some other trip on the waterway I'd stop by and see if we made it to the wall of walls—Tony Seaman's photo gallery.

This sort of thing is great fun, and I really enjoyed Tony. His kind of people add color, enthusiasm, zest to the game of life. A little bit ego-happy? Sure, but such fun-people to be with. Tony was much like my dear friend John Carzis who owns Hugo's in Cohasset Harbor—good restauranteurs, good people to be with—the enthusiasts of America.

I think back about John Carzis and the night Allen Chambers

had a dinner party for Preston Martin, president of PMI Insurance Company, at Hugo's. John Carzis had come to the table at my invitation, and he told Pres his philosophy of life.

"I'm an optimist, and at seventy-five I am still working on great plans," he stated in his thick, expressive, melodramatic and heavily accented voice.

"Believe me, Mr. Martin," continued John Carzis, "on the night before I die I will be planning for the future."

With this John Carzis thundered his fist on the table for emphasis, puffed out his full lips, shook his mighty mane, half-closed his eyes, swung his Greco-Barrymore head to me and said, "Jackie, I love you!" Then he kissed my wife, ordered a round of Irish Mist for the table, and departed for yet another victory.

Yes, this Tony Seaman reminded me of John Carzis and Tony, if you ever read these words, that's a compliment.

Engine Trouble

The alarm went off at 0500 and I found that Milt had not lost his touch with the galley. His noble breakfast was a delight—orange juice, fried eggs and bacon, coffee and chocolate chip cookies. According to our book of rules, considering that Milt did the cooking and served the chocolate chip cookies, I did the dishes. My, but that Ivory liquid soap is really super!

We had our lines aboard at 0600, and we idled at the dock awaiting the first crack of light. How stimulating it felt to be back on the bridge of *Islander* in the crisp cool of this North Carolina morning. I breathed as deeply as I could, time after time, and my lungs and head tingled with the refreshing feeling that can only come this way. The salt air seems to penetrate right down to the toes. Nothing makes me feel any better than being at the helm, on the bridge of *Islander* in the early morning.

The faintest ray of light cut the darkness and we were on our way, inching up the channel past the dock where huge piles of wood chips were heaped awaiting shipment into the stream, under the great Beaufort-Morehead City Bridge.

Our bridge was shipshape—binoculars, camera, charts, my log book, and two great mugs of steaming hot coffee. What a day this was going to be! We would cover at least 120 miles of waterway, if all went well.

We left Spooners Creek to starboard and worked our way up the waterway, cutting back speed when we came upon the several clam diggers who worked the shallow waters at the very edge of the channel, sometimes not more than fifty feet from our boat.

The sun was now out, warm and welcome, and Milt had the helm while I made notes in the log book.

Then something went wrong!

"Hey, Jack," startled Milt. "The port engine. We've lost power."

It was not terror in his voice but an expression of sheer astonishment and bewilderment.

"What the heck is happening? The port engine is out completely."

I popped up, looked over Milt's left shoulder at the console and, sure enough, the engine had quit but there had been no warning buzzer from the automatic system. The theory is that when the engine loses oil pressure the buzzer sounds on the bridge, giving the captain ample time to turn off the ignition switch before any serious damage can be done.

This was the case with *Islander* when last August over Cross Rip Shoals, between Falmouth and Nantucket, our line to the oil cooler on the starboard side let go. The buzzer sounded the alarm and I was able to shut her down quickly before any internal damage could be done to the engine.

But here—no pressure and no buzzer.

I literally flew down the ladder from the bridge. When I got to the cabin I looked at the other set of instruments on the lower console, but this was not necessary because the furious knocking of the engine told the story.

I cut the power, hollered to Milt, pulled away the furniture, ripped back the thick red wall-to-wall rug, and yanked open the hatch cover.

Smoke, thick oily smoke, gushed up from the bilge. I grabbed at the fire extinguisher which hung in its bracket by the lower console and stood by looking for flames.

It was a tense moment while I waited for fire to break out, but it did not. With the power down, the engine cooled and the smoke subsided.

Swansboro

Whatever our trouble, neither one of us was going to be able to fix it, so we started the starboard engine, put a wrench in the shaft of the port engine to prevent the shaft from turning and doing damage to the transmission, and set a course for Swansboro which appeared to be only three miles farther down the waterway.

I was really convinced that we could be able to make some minor repair to a hose line and we would be on our way before noon. That was an idle wish as it turned out.

Swansboro is a port of modest size on the west side of the waterway. Our guidebook brought our attention to a narrow-mouthed little basin as the first available in the Swansboro area.

"Holy hell, Jack," said Milt as we moved into the channel toward the Swansboro Yacht Basin. "You've got one foot on the right hand and two feet on the left hand," as I kept *Islander* in the thread moving ahead at about two knots, the starboard engine working well. "This is a small boat basin and no way are we going to fit. The depth looks to be four or five feet, so you better keep it on course."

Fortunately *Islander*, beamy old lass as she is, squeezed through the handle into the frying-pan-shaped basin.

Milt and I stood on the bridge of *Islander* and looked over the scene in the basin.

"No way is this the place we've got to be, Milt," I said. "There's nothing in here over twenty-five feet."

Milt spotted a couple of old-timers in an eighteen-foot aluminum open boat, and we pulled alongside and told about our need for a first-class mechanic.

"Well, I'll tell ya," said one of the old-timers, "we don't have any mechanic over here, but the next dock down the waterway—that's John Willard Dudley's Gulf dock—they got a good man."

So, we backed and filled, using our one engine, and slowly turning *Islander* in tight quarters moved her back up the handle of the frying pan into the waterway and along to the next pier.

As we glided forward, we caught our first look at Bruce Guthrie, 6' 5", 260 pounds of him, dinosauring his way down the dock waving us off.

"Come 'round inside the bar," he cautioned. "Keep inside, nice and easy," and he took our line and tied us down. "Those 'vironmentalists from the state won't let us dredge out that bar and it sure is hurtin' our gas business. Big boats don't want to come in here and risk hittin' the bar."

A knock in the engine is not always a man's best friend, and this was pretty obvious thirty minutes after docking.

Our friend Bruce Guthrie got the engine hatches open and called in Donnie, the local master marine mechanic. Donnie was in the constricted area between the hull and the engine tapping and was turning and squinting. Bruce, with those size fourteen gumboats that he referred to as shoes, was by now stomping grease over the teak deck.

"Yes sah, ya got some troubles, big troubles right cher," said Donnie as he pointed to our big 265-horsepower Palmer engine. "Sounds like ya threw a rod and maybe scored the cylinders, but before I say anythin' for sure I want to talk to John Willard."

Now John Willard is the king of this little mechanical domain, and he is the son of Willard Dudley, the owner. The elder Dudley seems to be in a position of respect and control, and he works pretty hard and long hours at the combination Gulf station and marina, but the final say on most mechanical matters seems to filter directly over to son John Willard Dudley.

Later on that day, a big discussion took place in the cockpit of the *Islander*. Bruce; Donnie, who really was turning out to be a real crackerjack of a mechanic; two or three of the local sport fishing captains; and John Willard Dudley. The diagnosis was —new bearings all around.

John Willard, true to his reputation for taking command of the situation, telephoned the distributor in Charlotte and was assured that the necessary parts would be delivered by bus to nearby Jacksonville, North Carolina by 0800 on the next morning, that was Friday.

This gave Milt and me an opportunity to relax a bit and to try to clean up the boat somewhat—which was in itself a difficult job because, among other things, while Donnie was inspecting the innards of the engine he, of course, had to erect and build a big wooden A-frame in the cabin, and from that he hung his chain fall which lifted the engine from its bed and suspended it in a free pendulum position.

What a heartbreaker it was to have to look at our clean Bristol condition *Islander* and see the mess that had occurred. Oil smudges on the teak, paper and tarpaulins all over the cockpit, an ugly wooden A-frame in the middle of the salon, and a greasy old engine dangling from a chain. But clean it up we did, or at least as best we could, and then it was off to a dining experience in Swansboro.

It had been recommended that we visit Captain Charley's Seafood Delight down the highway, over the bridge and into downtown Swansboro, which really wasn't much. But if the town wasn't much, or the outside of Captain Charley's wasn't much, the food made up for it because, believe me, it was about the best seafood dinner that I think I have ever had in my entire life. We had enjoyed Tony's Sanitary Fishmarket the night before when we

Donnie straddles our engine and his expression tells the story.

ate in Morehead City, but without any disrespect to Tony, Captain Charley's was even better. It was a little on the home style, much on the homespun, and most of the patrons were real locals who came there for the delight of Captain Charley's seafood. If you are ever in the area, we recommend it. And as for the menu, everything seemed to be sensational and enough to tickle the palate of the most discriminating gourmet.

Further Delays

The next day was a busy one aboard the *Islander*. The parts arrived at the Jacksonville bus depot on schedule, and reliable Donnie was on hand to get them and to start repairing the engine. It looked to us like it was going to be a long job, so Milt and I borrowed Willard Dudley's 1968 Chevy and drove the twenty-two miles back to Morehead City to get a few marine parts we needed for the boat and, also, to see if we could find my camel's hair cap that I had left on the hook at Tony's Sanitary Fishmarket the night before.

We not only got the marine parts but also found the hat. Four hours later when we arrived back at Willard Dudley's Gulf Station-Marina, Donnie was still up to his elbows in engine parts and he told us that "no way are we going to make it by tonight—maybe tomorrow." But tomorrow came and tomorrow went, and every time that we thought we'd have a departure schedule, Donnie found something else that had to be either clamped or tightened or fitted or adjusted or replaced.

In order to help while away this unhappy Saturday, Milt and I got a sort of twisted pleasure from hanging up the framed print that we had purchased in Morehead City a few days prior. It was a print framed in teakwood that we affixed to the wall of the lower salon of the *Islander* with bright, shiny brass screws. It was entitled "Marine Disasters Off the Outer Banks of North Carolina," and as we looked at it, we could only think that in our own little world the port engine of the *Islander* should perhaps be added to this long list of marine disasters of North Carolina.

And the work went on: Donnie, his consultants, the ever-present Bruce Guthrie, with an occasional visit from Willard Dudley or John Willard.

And the decision was made: John Willard stated that it was going to be impossible to finish the work on the *Islander* until he got more parts—next week.

Back to Boston

We decided to take our decision-making process back to Captain Charley's Seafood Delight where, over a sizzling plate of broiled scallops, we decided to catch a flight back to Boston in the morning, report back to our respective jobs, and come back and fetch *Islander* when she was again seaworthy and humming and purring.

It was with a sizable note of sadness that we climbed out of our seagoing attire and back into our business suits and trench coats and, with jam-packed suitcases still laden with the clothing we had brought to Houston for the national convention, headed down the dock for Willard Dudley's Gulf Station and the ride that would take us to the airport in Kinston, seventy miles away.

What a razzing we took from the fishermen on the dock who had gotten to know us over these past two days.

"Ya look like a pair of city slickers," was the chorus as we turned our back on *Islander* and started up the dock. This, indeed, was a surprising end to what was going to be a 465-mile run from Morehead City to Jacksonville, Florida. The distance covered from Morehead City to Swansboro was twenty-two miles, and that just really wasn't what we had in mind for Phase III of the cruise of the *Islander*.

We really had enjoyed the folks we had met. They were pleasant and friendly, yet not to excess. These North Carolina folks had a degree of reserve, yet were able to show a warmth that

Catching fish is big business at Swansboro.

made us feel completely at home. Both Milt and I knew that if we ever again travel the waterway we most certainly would stop in at Willard Dudley's Gulf for a load of gas. We knew that we would like to see Donnie and Bruce and John Willard, Willard Dudley, and the two Boston terriers again. As sad as the two or three days had been, sad and disappointing, this group at Swansboro, we knew, had done their best.

When we got back to Boston, we did our very best to try to explain the problems of the engine to John Reardon, but neither Milt nor I really felt that John, a much better mechanic than either one of us, really believed that what happened wasn't somewhere related to something that either Milt or I had done wrong.

The closest that we ever got to figuring out what really happened was that the belt on the salt water pump had given way because of some fatigue, causing the engine to drastically overheat and "scramble up the innards."

We kept in touch with John Willard on a daily basis for the next week or ten days and gave him the OK to haul *Islander* in order to realign the shaft and to make some other necessary adjustments. While she was hauled, we also decided to ask John Willard to have the boys put on a coat of bottom paint, so as to protect her for the rest of the winter.

November was fast disappearing and the weather in New England was getting cold, darn cold, and it was kind of tough for us working a seven-day-week in the Boston area and at the same time thinking of *Islander* down at her temporary home base in Swansboro, North Carolina. I checked my schedule on a daily basis and, with the pressures of the job, there was no way on this earth that I could see any time for me to shake loose and get to Swansboro, so I asked John if he could work something into his schedule.

A New Crew for the Islander

When the call came from John Willard that "*Islander* is all OK and ready to head south," John started working in earnest to try to find a crewmate for the journey.

He called me at my house one night early in December and said, "How about Frankie Partsch? Do you think Frankie would go?"

Frankie has been one of our oldest friends, someone with whom John and I grew up in Sand Hills thirty-five summers ago, when we were all high-school students. Frankie is a fine mechanic, has

John checks over the charts below Swansboro.

a great knowledge of boats, really has the spirit and love for adventure. So we knew that if he could get away from work, he would love the trip.

Frankie immediately was caught up in the thrill of the planned voyage. He called his boss, Tom Matthews, and Tom, great guy that he is, urged Frankie to "take the time off—go, don't worry about anything, we'll take care of your accounts while you're gone."

So Frankie agreed to go, but when John said, "We'll fly down to North Carolina and pick up the boat," Frankie rejoined with, "You fly if you like. I'll take the bus and I'll see you on the dock."

Frankie is an unusual guy in that he, a former Seabee in World War II and a spirited character if there ever was one, has a fear for flying that really is something else. And so, no way is he going to get in an airplane, even to get to *Islander*.

So the plans were made. John and Frankie about ready to leave for the *Islander* during the first week of December, 1976. I think this three or four day period was about the saddest that I ever could have because my heart really was on the *Islander*, and I would have loved to have been with the two of them. Here my long-planned trip was being decimated and interrupted, but responsibility of the job in this particular instance had to come first. In a company the size of ours, during the wild season we were in, it made sense that one of us had to mind the store—either John or me—so this was John's turn to go.

PHASE IV

SWANSBORO TO CHARLESTON

John's account of the trip from this period on was well done, interesting and accurate, so I recount it here in much of the original form in which he gave it to me upon his return. These are his words:

When I arrived at New Bern Airport, Steve Griffin was on hand to meet me.

"John Willard said for me to be here," said Steve.

"How's that engine sounding?" I asked.

"I understand from John Willard that it's just fine," answered Steve.

An hour later at dockside I had met and talked to Willard Dudley, the father; John Willard, the son; Donnie, the mechanic; and Bruce Guthrie, the great and large helper.

The report was that everything was just fine but to be on the safe side I decided, while waiting for Frankie's bus to come in, to check out as much as I could.

Both engines turned over healthily. It was nice to hear them sounding so hale and hearty.

I did some work on the water pressure pump to try to stop the pulley from slipping. I removed the pump, filed the bore of the pump pulley and slipped a brass bushing between the pulley and the shaft, reassembled it and it was again as good as new.

I then tried the Onan generator. Wow! Exhaust filled the cabin and no water came out of the stern pipe. That meant removing the exhaust hose. What a job that was, with Donnie crawling in the tight bilge area and with me fetching and passing in the tools.

While at it, we finally got the belt tightened and this whole act took us well into darkness.

Bruce brought word down to the *Islander* that Frankie had called from some bus depot somewhere with word that he would be at nearby Jacksonville, North Carolina by nine o'clock in the evening, so I was at Trailways depot at the appointed hour.

What a pleasure it was to see Frank's happy, smiling face come at me from amidst the crowd getting off the bus.

We drove back to Swansboro in Willard Dudley's 1968 Chevy and planned for an 0600 departure for a run we hoped would take us 500 miles south to Jacksonville.

Wow, was it cold! Ice on the boat. Maybe fifteen to twenty degrees. The natives said it had never been so cold! But inside, with the heaters working plus a little help from some of Turner's private stock, we thawed out long enough to get into our sleeping bags.

We were off the dock by 0645 and an hour later were off the firing range. And, it was good we reached there when we did because the big sign on the side of the waterway announced: "No passage between 8:00 A.M. and 5:00 P.M."

The Marines must have great concern for traveling boaters and would hate to drop a shell on any sleek craft like, say, the *Islander*, we quipped.

Later that morning we saw our first pontoon bridge, and what a wonder of the bridge engineering world that was. We made all kinds of pictures of this weird, water-crossing device, impressed with the genius of the designer.

By noon we had come abeam of Wrightsville Beach and had a chance to see the first-class marina at Whiskey Run.

The run below here was really sensational—something right out of the Amazon jungles with the waterway appearing to run in a trough under huge, overpowering trees heavy with moss and vines.

Another Delay

Ma Gregory's Marina at Shallotte, North Carolina was one of these waterway paradises that we would prefer never to see again. This marina was off to the right side of the waterway and as it did not look too brisk, we consulted our marina guide and went off to the right up a narrow creek to Carters' Marina. One look was enough, so it was back to Ma's—a mistake.

Old Ma, in her top side of her sixties, was in charge because her husband had just had a heart attack. As it was, Ma was crippled with arthritis, so I took the nozzle from the Texaco pump and let her rip.

Something didn't feel right, so I splashed some gas on the dock. Water! The gas was mixed with water! Ma had a leak in her tank.

Frank looked at this freak occurrence with amazement. "I don't believe it," he said.

Old Ma Gregory said, "Impossible!" until we hosed a liberal amount into an empty quart tonic bottle. The water settled on the bottom and the gas went to the top—a 50/50 mix.

Such a problem, and it could only be solved by pumping the starboard tank dry which must have had seventy-five gallons aboard by this time.

A near-frozen audience started to assemble as Frank jury-rigged an old electric pump he found up in Ma Gregory's yard, attached it to a garden hose and started pumping the watered gas out of the tank of the *Islander* into a big galvanized wash bucket.

Ted Kenyon and his wife Teddy, traveling in a big sailboat, were nearly completely frozen in the fifteen-degree evening as they emerged from their cabin to say, "Sorry for your trouble."

They were a pleasant couple, perhaps in their mid-sixties, who had traveled the waterway before, but they stated that "we have never been so uncomfortably cold before."

We suspended the pumping operation for a breather after Frank and I had toted twenty or thirty swishing gallons to the dumping ground in the sand by Ma's marine railway.

The Kenyons, Frank and I huddled up to the stout heaters in *Islander* and had a pop or two to get the blood moving again.

It turned out that Ted had founded the very famous Kenyon Instrument Company which is a quality word among boaters and his wife, Teddy, was herself no less distinguished because she had been a test pilot for Grumman Aviation.

Now deiced, we went back to the dock and continued sloshing gas from our sometimes sparking makeshift pump into the wash bucket and on up to Ma's sandbox.

Ken Touros, of New York joined the Kenyons and us as we finished the job, warmed up a bit, ate quickly, said, "Good sailing to our new friends" and crawled almost desperately into our sleeping bags.

Sometime in the cold black of that night the heaters cut out, so Frank—a Seabee to the hilt—slipped ashore, found the master fuse box and inserted a penny between the fuse and the connector making a circuit, plugging us back in the electric stream, then it was back into the sleeping bags for dreams of polar bears, Eskimos and icebergs.

By 0630 we were again on our way and now we kicked ourselves when only a fifteen-mile run below Ma Gregory's frigid dock we spotted the Little River Marina, an attractive-looking place we could have made with another hour of cruising—but better luck next trip.

Raw Cold on the Waterway

Another hundred or so miles down the waterway Frank and I had just about had it.

"I can't remember being so wet and so cold," declared Frank. "At least in World War II we were on Guadalcanal in the South Pacific and warm."

Frank admits it's "cold on the bridge."

"We'll never make Charleston tonight. Let's tie up at the next good place we can find."

That's how we got to Jim Leland's Texaco dock at McClellanville, South Carolina. Not much. Lots of shrimp boats, a general store, and some real nice people who shared the cold with us. Especially Jim Leland. He started his marina with nothing and, working with a really limited bankroll, is building a small but well-organized business.

Here we met the Doanes from Marion, Massachusetts, a family of three who, like ourselves, were shivering and shaking from the raw cold of the waterway evening. In spite of the trembling from the frigid night we toasted "good health and long life" to the elder Mr. Doane who, the day before, had reached his seventieth birthday. They would spend their winter in Florida and return to Marion for the summer season.

Then there was the *Optimist*, a fifty-six-footer of ancient vin-

Guardian of Frying Pan Shoals, off Shallotte Inlet gets some yard work.

tage which, now equipped with a pair of new diesels, would be used for daily fishing trips out of Fort Pierce, Florida before returning to Atlantic City, New Jersey for the summer season there. The four senior citizens taking the old *Optimist* south were partially warmed by their small electric heaters, with the chills somewhat resisted by plastic storm window coverings. But we were to see *Optimist* again at Charleston, after they had lost their pressure and scrambled one of their new transmissions.

The next morning was vital to us as we wanted an early, early start because we hoped to make Savannah, about 150 miles downstream, so we needed every second we could muster.

It was ink-black as we set our course at the eerie, bone-chilling hour of 0530. It was easier running the waterway in darkness than I ever would have suspected. After a few minutes our eyes became adjusted to the shadowy outlines of the shoreline and, using the

Getting across the Waterway is not always by bridge.

little hand chart-light that Milt had brought aboard, we could check off our marks that we easily picked up with our searchlight.

I think this was the highlight of the entire trip because this was adventure, with *Islander* purring on and working well. Then dawn came up and it broke out as a bitterly cold but beautifully sunny day. We were on the bridge, drinking coffee, happily half-frozen.

Engine Trouble — Again

I was at the helm. The port engine didn't handle right. I couldn't control it with the throttle. The buzzer alarm went off. I leaped down the ladder from the bridge, cut out the engines, pulled back the red rug, flung open the hatch, and smoke!—just like Jack had reported on our earlier voyage.

Trouble! We had fainting hearts. We felt crushed. For over

Frank puts her dockside at Charleston.

200 miles the engine, supposedly fixed at Swansboro, had acted fine—then crash all around us.

"It's got to be a connecting rod," guessed Frank. "Let's tie down the shaft and move her on."

I checked the chart and our closest port was going to be Charleston, South Carolina, a few easy hours at reduced speed.

"Keep it at six knots, Frank," cautioned John. "No sense pushing now. Let's just hope that we can find a mechanic who likes Palmer engines."

So it was a slow, very cautious and sad run to Charleston with our heavy mood lightened for a moment when we came up on Fort Sumter, the historic Charleston Harbor fortress that Union Major Robert Anderson had guarded so stoutly at the outbreak of the Civil War.

Islander waits for a new engine at winter quarters in Charleston.

We saw the tourist sight-seeing boat *General Beauregard* at the dock, and we knew that visiting Fort Sumter must be big business in season.

Shorty, at the Charleston Municipal Dock, was friendly and solicitous and, after the introductory stories were exchanged, he made arrangements for us to maneuver over to the nearby dock leased by Carolina Marine.

This was my first meeting with Drummond Farley, graduate engineer, a former condominium builder who had bitten the dust in 1974 like so many other builders.

Now he was into a new career with a neat, well-equipped machine and repair shop right on the Charleston docks.

It was now pretty obvious that our trip was over, at least for awhile. We called Jack with the dispiriting news. Frank went down to the Trailways station, and I stayed with boat and engine to await diagnosis.

A day later I had the verdict. The engine was scrambled eggs and the trick was to find a replacement engine—a Palmer for the port side.

"Seeing as how Palmer is out of business and doesn't make engines any more, this is going to be quite a challenge," I told Drummond.

So Drummond agreed to undertake the challenge and I was off to Boston to return to work.

After I talked to Jack when I returned there was no doubt in my mind what was going to happen. We were going to get that engine either fixed or replaced, and *Islander* was going to move on to Florida sooner or later, one way or another. The log of the *Islander* was not going to say "finis" at Charleston.

The daily reports from Drummond Farley were like Walter Cronkite's news bulletins. First he did find an engine. Then he didn't find an engine. First he could rebuild it, then he couldn't. First he found a dealer in New York City who had bought up the inventory when Palmer folded, then he didn't have our size, style and color.

A New Engine

It was now a week before Christmas. We felt we had to do something to get off dead center. The wheel had turned and the arrow was pointing at a new Chrysler 440-cubic-inch, 330-horsepower gas-propelled engine, and considering that our starboard engine was more than half or more expended, we made the big decision.

Naturally, price was a great consideration when discussing the problem, but the *Islander* at a dock in Charleston with only one working engine was not exactly what we had in mind, so Drummond Farley ordered the twin Chrysler, 330-horsepower, 440-cubic-inch engines from Bob Stanton at Norfolk Drydock and Shipbuilding, a Chrysler Marine distributor, and they were to be trucked posthaste to Charleston for immediate installation so we could be off by mid-Christmas week.

This was, however, the last we heard of "trucked posthaste" or "immediate installation" for a long time to come.

The truck driver took the engines home during Christmas, Drummond Farley's mechanic went on vacation, then the record-breaking-cold winter of 1977 set in and, as *Islander* was secured to an outside dock, very little in the way of "immediate installation" was forthcoming.

Actually, we understood because any son of South Carolina willing to work on an engine in a boat that was covered by ice and snow would have been a rare bird indeed.

So it was not until February 10, that we heard that "those twin Chryslers really sound good—come on down—we're ready for you."

This report ends Phase IV of the log of the *Islander* except to say Jack and I had some fast and furious readjustment meetings in his third-floor office at our Conway Country Building at Hanover as we tried to pry loose the time for the next phase in the log of the *Islander*.

Our final plans were that I would go down to Charleston on the seventeenth to work out any engine problems with Drummond Farley. Jack, his wife Patti and their daughter Carol would follow the next day, then my wife Mary and my son John would join us on the twenty-second at Jacksonville.

So, after our nine-week pause (incredible when you look back on it) the cruise of the *Islander* was about to recommence.

End of John's narrative.

PHASE V

CHARLESTON TO FORT LAUDERDALE

It was a raw cold February 19, when Patti, Carol and I arrived at Charleston Airport. We stepped from the plane looking for John who was to meet us.

There he was, wearing a new grey wool cap, head above the crowd.

"Hi, Jack," he greeted. "I want you to meet Drummond Farley."

"So you are the famous Mr. Farley," I cracked as I shook hands with the grinning, heavy-set, black-moustached proprietor of the Carolina Marine Services.

"How's the *Islander*?"

"Just great, Jack," said John. "We had our sea trials in Charleston Harbor late this afternoon. The engines are perfect and she gets up on a step at 2500 revolutions."

"Yeh, you fellows are all set to go—she should get you there," beamed Drummond Farley.

"Great—then it's 0600 tomorrow," I said, and we were off to the docks at Carolina Marine, all of us eagerly anticipating the long trip that lay ahead.

John and I made our peace with Farley, and I am sure he looked at our check approvingly when he noted that it was "certified."

As we left Drummond's dockside machine shop, John pointed

out the remains of our engine which were scattered or heaped on an iron pile.

There was the transmission, manifold, carburetor and header, heads, assorted pumps, pulleys, filters, connecting rods, well burned-out risers and a broken crank shaft. John then took particular pains to point out the hole in the block where the connecting rods ripped through the cylinder walls.

Yes, good-bye, old friend. You served us well, but not well enough.

And now it is on to the new and, if Drummond Farley is correct, our two new 330-horsepower Chryslers will propel *Islander* for "about 2300-2500 hours."

Quick figuring, and that comes out to about five years of heavy cruising. So we look ahead to the year 1982—and in these five years such wonderful places we will go.

Under Way Again

Islander—it's up, up and away!

And that's the way it happened, especially when Mr. Big Ben clattered us into action at 0530. It was deep darkness when we walked the few hundred yards to the great red-brick Civil War Civic and Administration building for morning showers and freshening—clean, well-lighted.

By 0700 we had finished a gratifying scrambled-eggs breakfast and were on our way in the cool, heavy overcast of dawn.

I had wanted to see Fort Sumter and relive some of the moments of Walter Lord's historical account of the first shots fired in the Civil War, but Fort Sumter was now behind us and *Islander* was to move onwards—south!

The morning broke cool and chilly and Patti and Carol soon left the bridge for a gin rummy game in the warm cabin below.

John was at the chart station. I was at the helm when we had our first chuckle of the day. Two dolphins came alongside and started to play in our wake. They dove and glided and jumped, in and out of the soft waves of our wake, just like two surfers. They followed us for miles, sometimes leaving for a few minutes, but always coming back to play some more. Carol had loads of fun trying to photograph them, but they were a split-second flash and really did not have too much time for picture posing.

The waterway—and what a treat it was to be back on it again— unfolded, mile after mile. Low, piney country carpeted by swamp grass. Uneven shorelines, little islands, secret streams, occasional flocks of birds, sometimes a lone fisherman, and a bridge or two.

The only cluster of activity was the small navy repair yard at Young's Island where the Wadinalom River came on Oyster House Creek. It was interesting to see the old World War II LCU's tied alongside the dock while welders patched this and that. We wondered whatever their mission was these quiet days.

We proceeded on, but the presence of Uncle Sam was again within range as a gleaming white U.S. Coast Guard ninety-three-footer flashed her blue rotating warning light, and we knew something was up.

Two men in a rubber raft boat, powered by an outboard motor, set out from the ninety-three-footer obviously intent upon intercepting us.

I was alone on the bridge, but when I pulled back power to stand by for the boarding, John, Patti and Carol sprang out of the cabin.

"Routine inspection—that's all, just routine," said Coast Guardsman Don Gordon as he made fast his lines and clambered aboard.

We drifted on the South Edisto River between Alligator Creek and Raccoon Island as the Coast Guardsman did his thing. He gave us the full safety check, and it was with a pleasant sigh of relief that he completed his form, bid us well, and we were off again.

Carol's first bridge — Beaufort, S. C.

Beaufort's tall bridge could be seen from a distance and our waterway chart told us we were sixty-five miles below Charleston, a good run, six hours, eleven miles per hour, easy cruising.

Carol had been at the helm for several hours, with John charting courses, and when John allowed her to take the *Islander* under the high-bridge span, "My first bridge—I took the boat under my first bridge!" she exclaimed, thrilled.

Beaufort, from the waterway, was a picturesque Southern town. The architecture of the white buildings along the shoreline appeared to be from the Civil War period, and its waterfront marina was inviting. Perhaps we would stay there another time.

The huge U.S. Marine Corps Base, at Parris Island, is just below Beaufort, and we were sorry that it began to squall because the grey skies spoiled our picture taking.

The wind came from the east and packed in through the wide opening to the Atlantic through Royal Sound.

I thought of how many tens of thousands of young marines must have shipped out of Parris Island over the years and headed easterly through the same Royal Sound, bound for battlefields far, far away.

There was a heavy chop running but *Islander,* as always, performed well. Nevertheless, we were happy, especially Carol, who was at the helm when we slipped into the quiet, protected waters of Skull Creek which took us down to Hilton Head Harbor. It proved to be small and a disappointment. For years I had heard what a big deal Hilton Head was supposed to be.

It was not until eight miles farther along when we spotted the striped lighthouse at Harbortown—familiar to me because of Hilton Head sales brochures—that we found that Harbortown was the well-known development area, with its pretty harbor.

We cruised over and inspected the huge cluster of Hilton Head condominiums and the small but fine marina with all the large yachts, but it was late so we did not go ashore.

Soft Air and Palm Trees

Back on course we saw our first pelican at Marker 34 on the Cooper River and knew we were nearing the South. The air, for the first time, became soft. The sun was strong and John started taking a toasting on his well-exposed skull.

And then we saw our first palm trees, and we knew it was all true—that we were getting South.

The twenty-mile area between Hilton Head and Savannah twists and turns, very narrow in places, and at that period low tide, so it was "eyes on the fathometer at all times."

The two tightest spots were picturesque Ramshorn Creek that connected the Cooper River with the New River where we had a four feet reading at times, and Fields Cut where we took a bite out of a mud bank just before we made it into the busy Savannah River.

We could have proceeded eight miles up the Savannah to the gracious southern city and have dinner at the famous Pirates House which the waterway guide says has "23 unique dining rooms," but that would have meant backtracking in the morning, therefore we took our other option.

We crossed the Savannah River and followed the waterway course between Elba Island and Bird Island and followed the Wilmington River for five or six miles to the Thunderbolt Marina, a jewel of a place, just 115 miles and ten hours of easy cruising from Charleston.

Max Butler, the dock boy, tied us broadside to a handsome, well-maintained dock. The facilities were perfect—clean heads, clean showers, plenty of hot water and a first-class restaurant called "Tassy's Pier." The shrimp and seafood were superb! A highly recommended port of call on the waterway!

And Engine Trouble—Again

By 0700 Sunday, February 20, the *Islander* was again purring down the waterway, but as we approached Isle of Hope, eight miles downstream, our new warning bell sounded and we knew we had troubles.

"Dad, the bell is ringing," excitedly called Carol, as we shut down both engines. This time it was the starboard engine. A quick check showed no water in the expansion tank. This is a closed system and where the trouble was completely confounded us.

As good luck would have it, we were within a few hundred yards of the Isle of Hope Marina. Otto, the dockmaster, said, "Today's Sunday—no mechanics today!" So we called dear old Drummond Farley in Charleston and asked, "What does a guy do in a case like this?"

Drummond, thankfully, said, "Get a cup of coffee and relax. I'll be down there by noon."

Isle of Hope, Georgia, is beautiful. Carol, Patti and John take a stroll.

Such a feeling of frustration! Two brand new Chrysler 330-horsepower engines, and still we have mechanical troubles. But all was not lost as Isle of Hope is a charming place to visit.

The thousands of huge, old and gnarled oak trees heavy with grey and misty gypsy moss gave the place a mysterious William-Faulkner-feeling. The homes were neat and pleasant.

As it was Sunday, we looked for a Catholic church so we could attend mass, but the closest thing we found to activity was the Isle of Hope store where Bob Hendry, the clerk, told us about his plan to attend Annapolis after high-school graduation.

"But first I'm going to hike the Allegheny Trail—Georgia to Maine—and two buddies and I are going to try it next September," he said. "It'll take us four months with a fifty-pound pack, so we'll get to Maine in December or January."

Islander at Isle of Hope as Jack and Patti wait for Drummond.

John suggested that there just might be a few inches of snow in the area at the time, but the caution did not bother Bob.

"We're going to do it, and it will be a really good thing," maintained the young man.

I thought about it and said that was the same reason we are taking the *Islander* on the waterway to Florida: "Because we think it is a good thing to do."

Back aboard, our first visitors were Del McGowan and his dog Leo. Del was a local marine mechanic and judging his tentative diagnosis of our problem, a competent one.

"From what you tell me, it sounds like trouble in the heat exchanger—a bad weld by the manufacturer," he said.

Osmer Bailey bends over heat exchanger as John oversees the project.

It will be interesting to see what Drummond Farley says when he and his mechanic get here, I thought.

Before long Drummond Farley was on hand, having driven the 150 miles from Charleston, and he introduced us to Osmer Bailey—a thin, tall, angular youth whom it turned out was not only a fine mechanic but an exemplary young man.

Then the countdown began.

Osmer serpentined his bone-thin frame into the bilge area, checked all the hose connections, then got into the heat exchanger, removing it and taking it to the dock for pressure tests.

Otto, the dockmaster, was a great help in making various arrangements, but all the tests proved negative, so it was back to the engine room for Osmer.

Drummond pressurized the tank and Osmer, now on his back in the bilge and under the engine, found the problem—a leak in the manifold! A leak in the brand-new Chrysler Marine manifold!

Drummond Farley works on the riser.

Boy was John mad! This hairline crack, making so much trouble for so many people, was the result of a flaw in the casting which could have been caused by a number of reasons—a bad mix with the grit, an improper heating treatment, or some other foundry mishmash.

"They run tests on these things," said John, "but they missed this one."

It really is too bad when some person goofs in the manufacturing process, on not just a manifold for Chrysler but in anything, because someone suffers somewhere along the line.

Sometimes it's the sales department which causes the problem by screaming for a lower price for an item in order to make more sales and then manufacturing says, "The only way I can make the product at your price is to cut in quality." I do not know what the problem was here—poor foundry work, a mistake, or a call by management for lower price at the expense of quality—but John, Osmer, Drummond and I were darn mad about a defective part in a brand-new engine.

With the problem now diagnosed, the next trick was to find a replacement part.

Drummond talked about the Chrysler warranty and about getting a new part from Norfolk Drydock and Shipbuilding, the Chrysler distributor, but that would take at least two days, maybe more.

This was horribly discouraging news, but Otto saved the bacon by finding a manifold at the nearby Tidewater Marina.

Tidewater had the part—not exactly like the original, but close enough to do the trick. But it really was a thoroughly unpleasant place to do business. First of all, the place was "termited" by several of the local Sunday afternoon drunks, one of them being a youngish, high-pitched voiced, rather stupid person who dominated the scenario. Two or three others were local boatsmen customers, all well on their way to no-no land. The mechanic, decent enough I suppose, fought through the surrounding senseless talk long enough to listen to Drummond's problem. But when Drummond told his Chrysler warranty story, the mechanic became a one-time-only businessman and refused Drummond the courtesy trade discount on the $148 item.

"Never mind," said Drummond when we were back in the car with Pat Wooten, his fiancee and office manager, heading for the *Islander*, "I'll catch one of these Tidewater boys heading up the waterway some day."

Back on the *Islander*, now growing raw and cold, the temperature dropping like a plumbline, Osmer worked steadily on fitting gaskets, lengthening and adjusting hoses and getting the air out of the fresh water system.

Finally, close to 2100, it was done!

We enjoyed Schenley on the rocks—all seven of us!

Farther South and More Cold

By 0530 our crew was up—Patti had oodles of juicy scrambled eggs on the table, and we were ready for the waterway before 0700.

The first break of light was sheer rapture. The sky in the east started to show orange and red, fighting to push away the jet black. The first light danced on the calm Skidaway River. I watched a black mass of grass float downstream. Then I could see fish make pools and ringlets as they broke water. A clump of trees on the other side was silhouetted. The light became stronger, the river was calm, but it shone in the morning's brightness.

Patti stood on the afterdeck of *Islander* enjoying the scene with me. It was a truly reverent moment as God began His day.

The engines turned over efficiently, proving that Osmer had done his job well, and we slid into Skidaway Narrows, a place that the waterway guide called a "tortuous and winding passage" of great concern, but today we had a half-tide and so were able to enjoy the landscape punctuated by a view of the quiet seaside houses of Vernon View and Possum Point.

A while later we traversed Hell Gate which connects the Vernon with the Ogeechee, and this was indeed a short but testy passage with really tight water, but we took advantage of a range on our stern and came through just fine. The guide had called this "Hell Gate, a place of broken propellers and twisted shafts," but John's able eyes at the chart station took us through.

When we pulled out of the Ogeechee into what is called the Florida Passage, we felt something magical was going to happen—but it did not.

The cold was bone-chilling, well below freezing, and the southwesterly wind was coming in at fifteen knots!

We passed a tug pushing a long tow at Kilkenny Creek, and this was the first boat we had seen for the day and the last we would see for six hours and almost seventy-five miles.

The waterway in this area really is lovely, but how desolate.

Saint Catherine Sound was rough, and we took water on the bow and spray on the bridge. Johnson's Creek was out of this world, and we could see over tens of miles of sawgrass.

Sapelo Sound was again rough and whitecapped, but we enjoyed going past Blackbeard Island which, according to legend, was one of the many places where Pirate Blackbeard had buried treasure and where he had been hung as well as beheaded. President Teddy Roosevelt, back about the turn of the century, had this beautiful island declared a national preserve.

We continued. Still sunny but stone-cold! Nature unfolding, in her magnificence, mile after mile after mile. Waving grasses bent by the winds, lit by the sun. Waterway frothing with wind-blown chop, but the beauty was enhanced to an nth degree.

Amelia Island Plantation

We saw vacation and fishing lodges complete with private docks as we came north of little Simons Island, and late in the day when we got to the south end of Simons Island, just past the lift bridge,

Patti enjoys the passage of Saint Catherine's Sound between Savannah and Jacksonville.

John and Jack watch the channel above Fernandina, Florida.

we saw the Golden Isle Marina, our first marina in eighty-five miles, but we did not stop here but set out for Fernandina to the south.

This was a pleasant little port, small but adequate public marina, sufficient services, and a nice wide and comfortable main street with a variety of shops that serviced the shrimp boaters, the folks at the pulp mills, the summer vacationers, and the ever-coming conventioners who visited nearby Amelia Island Plantation.

Patti and I had visited the Plantation several years ago for a real estate meeting with our RELO group, and we had found the place a noteworthy resort condominium community with hundreds of well-structured units, a great plan, a fine golf course, all the other amenities, plus a pure sand, five-mile long, almost deserted beach.

But business was bad and the place was teetering on disaster's edge waiting for either a financial miracle or a surge of red hot, well-heeled buyers—or preferably both.

That evening at dinner at Fernandina's fine steak house, The 1886 Restaurant, we asked Michael, our waiter, how things were at Amelia Island Plantation.

"They still have big troubles, but I understand a new group from Dallas has taken over," replied Michael.

It is easy to see how important the Plantation is to the economy of the area as, while we were dining, a large party of twelve men came in for dinner followed shortly after by a party of ten men.

Both parties were from business meeting groups staying at Amelia Plantation, and neither party was with the same meeting.

Dense Fog, A Bound Propeller, and Worn Zincs

By 0530 when we awoke the air was filled with the thick acrid smell from the nearby wood pulp mills that clanked engines and spewed smoke on a seemingly continual basis. The smell was so vile and offensive that Patti suggested we get underway early and have breakfast on the waterway.

Early morning on the waterway was all that John and I could handle, however, as we miscalculated the denseness of an early morning ground fog that forced us to cut our speed back to only a few knots and to run on compass.

We bit mud one little old time, but otherwise came through it with nothing more seriously wrong than an unravelled nervous system stretched to the length as we wondered what tug would be coming upstream pushing how many barges as we groped in the fog.

By 0900 the fog was dissipated and we were closing in on the marina at Jacksonville Beach when the whole boat shuddered. We had hit something!

John cut the power, hauled back into neutral. We looked

Islander visits Jacksonville Beach as John and Carol indicate, "So what else is new?"

astern. Something was chopped up in the water—orange, white pieces. It could have been anything submerged— maybe a sunken crab trap. Our port propeller was partially bound.

Well, with a partially disabled propeller or a bent shaft there was only one thing to do. We proceeded at low speed along to the Jacksonville Beach area where we had heard there were repair facilities.

Buz Palmer at Beach Marine, on the east side of the waterway before the bridge, made a trial diagnosis of the problem and in what seemed like seconds had us in the sling of a huge travel-lift and our sixteen-ton vessel was hoisted high up out of the water. There was the trouble—a twisted yellow nylon line wrapped tightly around the port prop.

The line was weighted, which was what caused it to float just below the surface.

"Probably a water-skier's towline, or maybe someone was using it for crab pots," surmised Buz.

John was under the boat with David, the mechanic, inspecting for other damage when he noticed that the four zincs that we had, two on the shafts and two on the rudder blades, had suffered badly from electrolysis.

"They were new last December at Swansboro," said John, amazed at the pitted deterioration.

"Lots of things could have done it," shrugged Buz. "Electrolysis could have come from your own boat, another boat at the marina, or even from the marina itself. While we have you out of the water rather than just replacing the worn zincs, let me put two zinc plates on the transom. It should help with the problem and they are easier to keep an eye on for caution's sake," suggested Buz.

We agreed, and we really only lost a few hours and we now knew that all precautions possible had been taken.

John and I will never forget back a few years ago when the rudder became unglued and fell off the old *Ballyhoo* as we pulled into Provincetown Harbor one morning at 0600 after a nighttime cruise over from Scituate Harbor.

That time it could have been electrolysis that had eaten away the metal, causing it to fall to the ocean's floor—so we are aware of the electrolysis problem.

Finally the job was done, the bill paid, and by 1230 we were moving down the waterway.

For miles and miles (fifty of them before we docked for the night) we had seen spectacular sights, all of them making our efforts well worthwhile.

Areas like Cabbage Swamp, Spanish Landing, Tolomato River, all leading to the ancient American city of Saint Augustine, were each different and exciting.

Patti and I got a bit of nostalgic enjoyment out of seeing the twin towers atop the old Ponce de Leon Hotel in downtown Saint Augustine, because it was in this fine old place that we had stayed during part of our honeymoon twenty-three years and three weeks before.

The next stretch of waterway, running inside of Anastasia Island, took us to Rattlesnake Island, inside of Matanzas Inlet, where we ran in very tight water which was a result of sediment from the sea keeping ahead of the dredging operations.

To correct this, the Corps of Army Engineers is filling in and sealing the direct entry of the Inlet to the waterway and rerouting it by way of the Matanzas River which was the original entry to the sea before a great hurricane storm changed things around.

By the time we had gotten to nearby Marineland Marina it was almost 1700 and really not worth the effort to make the fifteen-mile run to the Flagler Beach Marina, so we tied down for the night and enjoyed first-class accommodations at the marina, walking over for a visit to Marineland itself and having a fine dinner at the Dolphin Restaurant which had been recommended to us by Bart, the dockboy.

When I told the hostess about Bart's recommendation, she joked, "That's nice, but it was not a hard choice for him to make as we are the only restaurant in the area."

John's Last Day

Dawn came and again by 0700 we were moving down the waterway towards Daytona, thirty-five miles distant, where John was going to say, "Good-bye," as he was catching a jet back to Boston. John really regretted leaving the southern-bound *Islander*, but, inasmuch as Eastern Airlines had fouled up Mary and John's reservations to Florida, my good friend decided he had best go home and join the family.

As much as I hated to see John go home, we knew that was how

The Waterway below Marineland was magnificent.

it had to be. Patti joked about my losing my security blanket which, in a way, really is true because my knowledge of engines, their design and functions is limited at best. Having John aboard, with his magic touch with a tool box, really keeps me relaxed.

John's last few hours aboard the *Islander*, for awhile at least, were going to be one of the great thrills of our trip south because the next three hours were something right out of Audubon's *America's Book of Birds*. The sun was bright, the weather balmy, and we saw thousands and thousands of birds. I only wish that my brother Bill, an avid bird lover and expert, had been able to have been along. Bill is a past president of The Audubon Society in his home city of Fort Lauderdale, and I remember pleasantly the many bird-sighting trips Bill has taken me on in the past.

As a matter of fact, I had invited Bill to fly up to Jacksonville, meet the *Islander* there, and take the trip south with us, but the demands of his busy law practice made this a "no-no."

This was our first look at some of the many little mangrove islands we were to see over the next few days—little half-acre or acre clumps of isolated growth dotting the waterway like a long string of pearls.

We all enjoyed looking at the two or three miles of waterway frontage of the Palm Coast area, one of those huge planned communities that have helped Florida grow. It was interesting to look on our charts at the honeycomb of man-dug canals pitting Palm Coast.

This community was of special interest to me because at one time we had been offered the Greater Boston sales and marketing package for the area but, as we were working with Point Brittany at Saint Petersburg at the time, we decided against Palm Coast. And, it was well that we did because their sales program fell apart shortly thereafter and we would have had to shoulder a large burden that we could well live without.

We understand that the sales program now is moving ahead. They have three entrances to the waterway. One of them, a main clubhouse entrance, is handsomely landscaped and the guidebook indicates Palm Coast is a hospitable marina which welcomes waterway wanderers like us.

The run down the Halifax River to Daytona was wide and wonderful, the homes on the east of the waterway now easily visible, every neat home with its own private dock. We could see Daytona bridges and a tall Daytona office building which, we were sure, must be a bank.

After miles among the swaying grasses and mangrove clumps, any building over a few stories high takes on massive proportions.

"The Daytona Municipal Yacht Basin looks like the best spot for us to pull in," stated John after a studious period of consultation with both the guidebook and the chart. "Go under the third bridge then, and as Otto at Isle of Hope phrases it, 'Hook a right!'"

And "hook a right" we did, between a tricky little coral rock jetty, up a passage and into a truly beautiful yacht basin, a gas

Carol was a great helmsman, a new security blanket.

dock on the left, the dockmaster on a long pier to the right. Plenty of water and right on the downtown edge of the city of Daytona.

"Good-bye, John," we all called as he, clad in his blue, brass-buttoned jacket, shirt and tie, holding a suitcase, stepped off the *Islander* and headed for the cab stand, Daytona Airport and Boston.

"Well, Jack, there goes your security blanket. Good luck," quipped Patti.

A New Helmsman

So, soon the pattern for the rest of our trip started taking shape. Carol, for the most part at the helm, alternating occasionally with Patti, and I at the chart station calling off the courses and markings.

Much of the waterway here had limited depth, and the only real tight spot was in the Rockhouse Creek area, back of the Ponce de Leon Inlet, where again sands of the Atlantic caused the waterway to shoal.

But with Carol a steady hand at the helm, we cruised through without scraping bottom and came upon the community of New Smyrna Beach, fifteen miles below Daytona and obviously a mecca for shrimping. Lots of commercial activity here plus what appeared to be a fine yacht basin nestled under the extended balconies of an incongruous mid-rise apartment building or condo.

Then fifteen more miles through another paradise of nature, continually making this trip ever and ever more worthwhile, until we emptied out into broad Mosquito Lagoon, a ten-mile-long, two and one-half-mile-wide body of shallow water with one long, straight as an arrow, well-marked channel along the westerly side.

The open expansiveness of this glittering lagoon, bright in the sunlight, gave me a new feeling of inner flotation after having been so many miles in the more confining channels of other parts of the waterway.

Carol handled the helm with skill as Patti and I tried to identify the birds on the many small islands that packed the lagoon.

Coming down the lagoon, it was interesting to see in the far distance the massive building at the Kennedy Space Center—Cape Canaveral. This is reputed to be the most vast building in the world and there certainly was no chance of mistaking it, even from our distant vantage point.

The chart was completely correct in calling for caution as we approached a sharp right turn up the Haulover Canal that connects with the Indian River.

"This looks like a real sharp one," said Carol, "but where is the entrance? I can't pick it out at all."

We moved slowly, turning right, then all at once it popped into view—the entrance to the Haulover Canal, a short mile up between a long row of Australian pines.

Once in, it was a pretty passage and historically interesting also. We were told that in olden days, sailing craft supplying the upper coasts of Florida used the inland passage and were hauled overland at this vital connecting point.

It was now early afternoon, so we began thinking of a destination for the evening. Titusville was too near, Cocoa was just about far enough, but we decided to gamble on the daylight factor and, in spite of a wind that was picking up, to run for the well-recommended Eau Gallie Yacht Basin about fifty miles down the waterway.

This was another notable cruise. We could see the Space Center buildings on our left hand and could visualize the thousands of acres of orange groves that we knew were on Merritt Island, a part of which is now a national wild life refuge.

When we passed Cocoa we thought of the time Patti and I stayed there on that trip twenty-three years ago when it was such a small community—before space travel, that is.

It was just a few minutes before dark when we got through the Eau Gallie bridge and found the small but well-marked channel to the Eau Gallie Yacht Basin—one of the cleanest, nicest and best equipped small yards we have ever visited.

"We have been doing business here for eighty-five years," Yardman Jim Howell told us proudly. "The yard has a reputation for high-quality work and 'Bud' Threadgill, the owner, continues keeping it shipshape."

Stormy Weather

We were tired after 120 miles on the waterway and were very happy we had stopped here, especially with bad weather predicted. This front roared through Eau Gallie the next morning packing

COMPASS COURSE 180°

Now she makes the lines ready.

strong winds, skies like black mud and torrential rains.

Islander was safe and dry and the efficiently maintained yacht yard was the perfect place to weather it out. We were thankful we were not on the waterway trying to hold a course and pick out channel markers in the rain blanket.

By noon it appeared to me that the front had passed through, but Jim cautioned, "Too early to go yet, Jack—second section of the front is building now. Look at those clouds racing."

It looked too good to me, however, so I called for Patti and Carol to throw off our lines and I headed to the waterway. But as I started south again Carol came popping up on the bridge and exclaimed, "Look, Dad, it's getting all black again."

And black it was. It was just to the north and northwest, so I did a fast 180 degrees and was back in port ten minutes later when the wild weather started all over again.

By 1530 the storm had finally gone on its way and we were on a course for Vero Beach, about forty miles downstream. We wanted to tie down at Vero Beach before dark so on some of the well-marked, broad stretches of the Indian River we opened our new engines up to 3,000 RPM and were logging better than fourteen miles per hour, our fastest speed thus far. This was the maximum for us, for awhile at least.

A Pleasant Stay at Vero Beach

The chart indicated a series of twisting "S" turns slightly below the Pelican Island National Wildlife Refuge and the Wabasso Beach bridge but, as much as they concerned me, Carol—calm and cool—took them in stride and we passed through a Florida paradise.

Winding channels, soft easy curves, orange groves, sandy-beached islands, hideaway coves, playful porpoises, and even a little dock with a sign that said: "John's Island Groves. Stop at our dock and load up with oranges for your boat. Spend the night. Only $3.00 dockage."

Truthfully, we would have enjoyed the stopover, but we decided to reserve our visit for another day and we continued our sunset run down the Indian River to Vero Beach.

"What a pretty place," said Patti as we gassed up and docked down for the night. The marina was good-sized, clean as a whistle, and the dockboy, Gregg, was very considerate.

Bill Ayers on the *Hea Bill*, a fifty-six-foot Hatteras cruising yacht, paid us a visit and related that he and his wife made this luxurious new yacht of theirs a floating home, visiting various ports as the urge arose.

And John Abner, just as happy in his twenty-foot houseboat as the Ayers were in their Hatteras, told us he had lived aboard here at Vero Beach dock for three years.

"Most times I don't even go anywhere. But once in awhile, when I feel like a fish-feed, I go up above a bit and drop a line.

It's nice living here," said the amiable Mr. Abner who was perhaps in his high sixties.

The sun was now a red ball in the west, and it set over the masts of a dozen sailboats in the anchorage. The sky was red and then, at the end, the skies and the waters blended their colors to produce a misty purple. I had never seen that color before at sunset time.

Gregg, the dockboy, had told me that the shops at the beach were "just a few blocks up that way." Perhaps they were "just a few blocks" to Gregg, but to me it was the last mile because my back and hip muscles were really singing a dirge. Either the ladder climbing, the long periods of inactivity as we cruised, or maybe a "stiffening of the joints," as my grandfather used to say, had really slowed me down.

When we reached the beach area it was all worthwhile as it was a tidy, attractive and sophisticated area of shops, restaurants and motels all on a long, sandy ocean-front beach. It sort of reminded me, in a small way, of the grace and order of places like Worth Avenue in Palm Beach and Las Olas Boulevard in Fort Lauderdale.

We found a restaurant on the beach side called Jacob's Ocean Grille, and it really was a fun-place to have dinner. The decor was on the rustic side, with some heavy black wrought-iron pieces hanging from the ceiling over the largest round table I had ever seen.

"That table is supposed to be the largest of its kind anywhere, and it is all one piece cut from a Honduras mahogany tree," explained Jenney, our waitress, a very tall, blonde and pretty English girl, who was enjoying her second week in the States, the place she had chosen for her new home.

"I like it very much here in Vero Beach," she said. "I have family here. The only thing I don't like is that here at the restaurant there was another Jenney. So they told me it would never do to have two Jenneys here and I was renamed Marie."

Carol, Patti and I called her Jenney.

Feeling somewhat less muscle-twisted after dinner, we toured the area and window-shopped the fine stores but did not walk the "just a few blocks" back to the marina. We found the local cab driver.

Porpoises and Speedboats

Dawn broke over our inlet at the Vero Beach Municipal Docks, and it was a delightful dawn so we knew it was going to be a day of days and, with luck, we hoped to be at our destination—dockside at the Fort Lauderdale Municipal Docks on the New River—by nightfall.

Patti took the helm and I assumed the chart station as we resumed our trip down the Indian River. We had tried to be as quiet as possible so as not to wake Carol, who needs her sleep. She had been so really terrific on this trip.

Our porpoises were still with us and we had a ball watching a family of four of them riding in our wake, surfing and leaping. The game went on for twenty minutes or so. Such fun they had—we too—and our efforts to get pictures of them as they leaped were not completely unsuccessful.

It was most appropriate that one of the points of land that we passed was called Porpoise Point, so this water ballet show we were getting was a home-field effort.

Just below this area was a fascinating sounding spot called Starvation Point, and it had a well-marked channel, so again maybe we'll visit here another day.

As we approached Fort Pierce, fifteen miles downstream, Carol joined us on the bridge and took the helm as Patti went below to prepare breakfast which was later served on our "flying bridge dining room." Just picture the adventure of having orange juice, scrambled eggs, bread and a big mug of coffee while we proceeded south, at thirteen miles per hour, under soft sunny skies on our waterway home *Islander* out of Scituate, Massachusetts.

Fort Pierce has direct access to the Atlantic and, therefore, is a port of major importance for commercial traffic and sports fishermen. We had an added thrill here as eight outboard motorboats, their engines wide open, their young drivers with either earphones or noise suppressors on their ears, came roaring up river.

What a race! They, literally, were out of the water almost riding on the tips of their propellers. Several of them took advantage of the waves of our wake and gripped their wheels more tightly as they hit the wake and leaped out into space. What jumps! What thrills for us! First leaping porpoises, now ski-jumping speedboats.

Saint Lucie Inlet

Our dockside advisers had told us about several nice ports below Fort Pierce. There was Nettles Island, fifteen miles below on the east, on the Hutchinson Island side of the waterway, which had a full-service marina as a feature of this area, built as a large community housing complex.

And, four miles farther along, there was the Frances Langford area, an outstanding area of condominiums, restaurant and a marina, which is on the west shore with a deep, well-marked channel leading in from the waterway.

The third was the busy and exciting area at Saint Lucie Inlet. The entry here is very tight and Carol was careful to ride the stern range coming into the inlet. Out of the range line the chart indicated a foot of water.

The item that makes Saint Lucie so exciting is that first, it has an entry to the sea, even though it is said that it is shoally at best and, second, is the turnoff spot if one desires to cut across the vastness of Florida to the West Coast ports of Naples, Fort Meyers, Sarasota, Saint Petersburg, Tampa and beyond.

When I originally planned this waterway adventure, my idea was to take the turn here and proceed up the Saint Lucie River, across Lake Okeechobee, and out to the Intracoastal that runs the Gulf of Mexico-side of Florida.

I had intended to tie down at Maximo Moorings Marina near our condominium at Point Brittany at Saint Petersburg. But our condo was booked solid by members of our sales organization who had won sales prizes of one kind of another, so I thought of Fort Lauderdale instead and would save the excitement of crossing the Florida Peninsula for another day, another voyage on the *Islander*.

This was a busy inlet, boats fishing, others coming, going, crossing the waterway or moving up to Stuart, which their chamber of commerce calls "the sailfish capital of the world." This title is earned because of the close proximity of Stuart to the teeming Gulf Stream which is supposed to be only five or six miles offshore. The warm waters of the Gulf Stream affect our climate and are juicy with fish life—it is the natural glidepath of the majestic sailfish—maybe, pound for pound, one of the greatest game fish of them all.

Hobe Sound

An hour or less below the tricky Saint Lucie passage we entered Hobe Sound which is protected from the Atlantic Ocean by Jupiter Island, a seventeen-mile-long land area which stretches from Saint Lucie Inlet on the north to Jupiter Inlet on the south.

And what an area this is!

We entered a world of waterfront estates, each more splendid than the other, lush green golf courses, sculptured trees, large boathouses—a world of wealth. We were told that these folks were among those who moved north from Palm Beach when that land of the rich and very rich became a little too crowded for their tastes. They have built a fitting testimony to the free enterprise system here on Hobe Sound.

'Matter of fact, I was so intent on watching this scene that, for a brief second, I strayed out of the narrow waterway channel and kicked up some sand—hardly a recommended thing for a yacht captain to do.

It was here at Hobe Sound that we gave our ship's horn a loud blast to celebrate the crossing of the 1,000-mile mark on the waterway. That's 1,000 miles below Norfolk, Virginia and, from rough calculations, I guess we were about 1650 miles south of our home port of Scituate, Massachusetts—a long, exciting adventure indeed.

Leaving Hobe Sound we found Jupiter Inlet, another entry to the sea, a beehive of commercial and yachting activity and, among the four yards and marinas we saw, there seemed to be ample docking choice for the waterway-cruising person.

Palm Beach

The dramatic scenery of this day, beginning at Vero, continued unabated as we cruised Lake Worth Creek which would lead us to fabled Lake Worth and Palm Beach—truly a high point in our trip.

It was in this area that we saw the huge yacht *Cross Angle III* out of Billings, Montana and wondered just how the heck the captain had gotten a sixty-foot behemoth over the top of the Rockies to the ocean? We are going to have to look this one up in our atlas!

A short while later, we exchanged waves with the helmsman on *Rejoice*, a yacht out of Manchester, New Hampshire. I think I remember seeing this yacht in local waters.

A well-used, weather-beaten sailboat hailed us as we were nearing the entry to Lake Worth at North Palm Beach. Two men aboard, heavy-bearded, their boat encumbered with gear that seemed to be stashed and lashed everywhere, told us they were going to the Bahamas for a few years.

They really looked the part, and I'm sure would fit right into the local scene at Harry's Tropical Bar in some out-of-the-way island.

But they were doing their own thing—all of us on the waterway were—each in his own way.

"Hey, Pat, get a load of this marina," I said as I pointed to the sharp and neat public gas dock at North Palm Beach.

"Maybe you'd like to stop here to call the office," suggested Pat as I made mental plans for my daily conference call to the crew back in Conway Country.

"No, not yet. I think I'll wait 'til we get to the dock at West Palm Beach—let's make the call in grand style at West Palm Beach," I joked.

Memories at Palm Beach

The ten-mile run down Lake Worth to the Flagler Marina at West Palm Beach was a wealth of memories—some good, some sad, some regretful.

The happy ones concerned many earlier years when my mother and father used to vacation at a now long-gone hotel on Ocean Boulevard, Palm Beach at the point where Worth Avenue met the ocean. I remember well my visits with them and the wonderful times we had at the Palm Beach clubs, like Alibi, and a few others, the names of which escape me now.

My father was a lawyer, a sports editor and columnist for the old *Boston Record-American-Sunday Advertiser,* and he and mother always took a six-weeks vacation, or more, every winter in Florida.

He would vacation for two weeks, then write and file his daily column for the rest of the stay.

From his base here at Palm Beach, he would visit the dog tracks at West Palm Beach, the horse tracks at Tropical, Hialeah and Gulfstream, the various baseball spring training camps and have a wonderful time for himself, all the time writing interesting stories for his half-million readers back home.

Dad was always a great host and immensely enjoyed having us

visit him in Florida. And all our friends were always welcome, too.

I remembered those happy, generously openhanded years of my father as we cruised Lake Worth, but then I also thought of the winter of 1950 when Dad died at his beloved Palm Beach.

He had been sick at home so he had gone to Palm Beach for an extended stay. I was working on the paper then, writing boxing, doing the sports promotions, working on the wire for the Green Race Special and a few other odd jobs.

One day, late in January of 1950, Dad and Mother were attending daily mass at Saint Edwards Church in Palm Beach. Dad had another heart attack there and died a few days later.

The week that Dad died, Ben Levias and I were doing the Silver Skates Derby at the Boston Garden. We had 700 participants in the show, sold out the Garden with 13,900 attendees, and sold 713,000 copies of the *Boston Sunday Advertiser,* an all-time circulation record for the paper.

Dad had written "end all" or "finis" to an illustrious legal, writing, promotional and editing career here at Palm Beach, and it was so appropriate that a man as fine, moral and considerate as he would suffer his last attack in a pew of a church.

We had now come to an area called Peanut Island and I swung the bow of *Islander* to port and took her out to Lake Worth Inlet between Singer Island and Palm Beach.

Patti and I pointed out the little motel on the point at Singer Island that she and I had wanted to buy ten or twelve years ago.

Business at home in those days was no better than mediocre, and we felt a change in life style was in order. We thought we would like to settle in the Palm Beach area and run a business and a Singer Island real estate man showed us the place.

We were all set to make the move and went home to pick up the loose ends, sell the house and give away the business to anyone who would have it.

This was a big move, but we felt the time was right. The cash we had on hand would be enough for a down payment on the apartment-motel building which was priced at $86,000, a figure we thought was about right at the time.

I'll never forget the real estate man who showed us the place. He first showed us the unit from the street side, did an historical swing through the neighborhood, selling happiness and profit every minute of the way, then took us through the units, obviously saw how impressed we were, then pulled out his big guns and let loose with a cannon blast!

He took us over to a dock behind his office, helped us aboard his eighteen-foot outboard, and we raced to the inlet and inspected the property from the sea.

He had us in the palm of his hands. Had the man been a "harder closer," I am sure Florida would have been our home today!

On the bridge of the *Islander* this memorable day, Patti and I reminisced and told Carol about these stories, and she smiled with wide-open eyes, fascinated by the thought that she might have grown up in Florida rather than in Scituate and Cohasset.

"How come you didn't do it?" asked Carol.

We answered that there is a time for every decision and our time for this one was the day we inspected the property from the sea.

"You see, Carol," Patti said, "we went home with every intention in the world of selling the house, getting rid of the business and coming back to Florida in a few months, but it just didn't work out."

I added, "No it did not—I guess when we got home we got involved in family, business got better, we got more snarled up in responsibilities, sales, bills and record keeping. The time was when we were there. It would have been easier then because our responsibilities were so far away. But when we got home these things came in around us again—like the feeling of one day dozing free and easy on the grass and another being wrapped in a tight blanket in a closed room with the windows shut." Carol, I am sure, understood.

The years, however, have been kind to my business life. We have expanded, prospered and heaped responsibility upon responsibility upon the mortal frame.

I am sure that this unconscious search for freedom from responsibility is one reason that being free on the *Islander* on the Inland Waterway means so much. My old friend, Frank Partsch, said the same thing to me after having traveled with the *Islander* on the waterway.

"It's so different—sometimes beautiful, sometimes lovely, sometimes breathtaking, sometimes ugly—but always different. It gives me a feeling of being at peace."

Islander moved toward the Flagler Beach that separated Palm Beach from West Palm. Carol slid her nicely under the great masonry bridge and, as we moved toward the dock, she got up from her helmsman's seat and said, "It's all yours, Dad."

Business Crisis Intrudes

The real world seems always at hand—sometimes near at hand—because upon calling the office from the dock I found that an important piece of business, in which I was personally involved, was in dire straights.

The heavy hand of responsible action was now on the helm, and after one hour and thirty minutes and five long-distance calls, my stomach was churning like the fiery waters of a charging inlet someplace.

It was now getting towards midafternoon, and I asked my very capable secretary, Ginnie Brett, to "set up everybody on a conference call at 4:30. I'll get down to Lantana Boatyard by then and let's see if we can get this deal back on track."

So, shortly after four o'clock (1600 hours), I was back in a phone booth on a hot, baking pier at the well-kept Lantana Boatyard and Ginnie had all parties to the transaction on a conference call. One party was in Greenwich, Connecticut; another in Boston; and a third in Braintree, Massachusetts.

The call went on, and on; my stomach churned and churned; but the longer and more quietly we talked I could feel the deal drawing closer and closer together.

It was over! The crisis had been resolved because of my actions in those phone booths from those Inland Waterway docks. A deal had been saved, minds had been put to rest, and everyone had profited. I felt that I had, with some skill, done a good day's work, but it was tough to untangle the knots and get back in the mood of the Inland Waterway again.

Delray Beach

I was now tired. Carol had the helm and Patti was at the chart station as we came down from Lantana, past Boynton Beach, and down onto Delray Beach where we thought we might tie down for the night.

The Delray Yacht Club looked like a suitable spot, but at 6:30 (1830 hours) their dock appeared deserted, so we opted for the Del Mar Marina, a mile farther down the waterway—but what a mistake this was.

The place was poorly attended, the gas dock was locked, the yard was dirty and unkempt, and their heads, showers and so-called recreation room were filthy—disappointing for a marina which had taken an impressive half-page ad in the waterway guide, in which it had one-by-one recited the litany of its virtues and assets.

"Let's get out of here," I said. "We'll run the waterway at night and we'll tie down somewhere below, maybe Boca Raton or even Bahia Mar in Fort Lauderdale."

"No," emphatically stated Patti. "I'm too tired and too disgusted to do anything but have dinner, go to bed and get out of here in the morning."

"Tell you what," I said, "we'll get a cab and go uptown for dinner."

To add insult to injury, the cab didn't show up so, tired as we were, we walked the mile to town, but upon reaching the business district of Delray, we found a delightful group of first-class stores, a peaceful setting and a Grade-A restaurant called The Patio where Jimmy the busboy, a native of the area, told us, "you'd like Delray—quiet, lots of 'old money,' not like Boca Raton which is 'new money.'"

Our waterway guide informed us that Delray had been settled by Michigan farmers in 1895, and the "old money" was, I am sure, a testimonial to their thrifty ways and longevity. As to the "new money," I assume this referred to some Boca Ratonians who had arrived on the scene after 1895 and were not Michigan farmers.

For the first time we overslept and it was not until eight o'clock (0800) that we were about to get underway, but it was with no help from the now-present attendant at Del Mar Marina who leaned on a piling by the gas dock, gawked at us, never nodded, never said good morning, never offered to toss off our lines, but seemed only waiting for us to pull over to the dock so he could hand us the hose so we could pump our own gas.

Having had enough of this rare glittering jewel of the waterway, I moved out ignoring the creature who, now aware that he was not about to pump several hundreds of gallons that morning, turned, locked up the gas dock, and moved inland to a worn, overstuffed chair, I assume.

Florida's Gold Coast

Now, on to a better day; on to an adventure; because now we knew we were about to move down the waterway into a forest of "right on" architecture, tall condominiums, estates by the waterway, beautiful yachts, and into the very ribbon of one of the most affluent civilizations on earth—Florida's Gold Coast.

Nor were we disappointed!

Carol, Patti and I were amazed beyond belief as we looked at the physical majesty of some of these homes. Each architect or builder was not to be outdone! Every style was unique. Most were fabulous. Some were grotesque in their gold-plated abundance.

What a morning this was for us! We contrasted the unspoiled stillness of the Georgia Tidelands with this—a land of everything packed upon everything, all crying, "Stop—look at me—I am the greatest!"

The Boca Raton Club was majestic, and we proceeded carefully so as not to throw even a ripple of a wake into their dockage area. I pointed out the new Bridge Hotel where I recently had dinner with my brother Bill and his wife Edie, a great rooftop restaurant shared with two splendid dinner companions.

Then we were upon the Hillsboro Inlet, a place I knew well as a result of the many sports fishing trips I had taken out of here in other years.

I thought of the cover on our old, now out of print, "This is Conway Country" brochure which Pat Costello had so ably put together for me some dozen or so years ago. On the cover was a charging sports fisherman coming into this same Hillsboro Inlet chasing before all of the raw power of a following sea.

Pat Costello and I selected this particular picture, which I had taken, as the cover photo of our brochure. It was later to win a national advertising award. We did not bother to mention that the picture had been taken not in "Conway Country" but at Hillsboro Inlet, Florida.

I later found out about the superior Lighthouse Point Yacht and Tennis Club which has excellent facilities for accredited yacht club members arriving from the waterway. Too bad. I would have enjoyed exchanging club burgees with them—a Scituate Harbor Yacht Club for a Lighthouse Point Yacht and Racquet Club.

Very soon we were at Pompano Beach. We began recognizing familiar landmarks and spotted a good marina for another day— Sands Harbor Inn and Marina—well-kept, clean and efficient.

Fort Lauderdale

Lauderdale-By-The-Sea, the Commercial Boulevard bridge, the beginning of the most fantastic explosion of Gold Coast building in the sixties, the ocean-front towers of the world-famous Galt Ocean Mile.

Patti and I knew this area well and, as we came down on the Oakland Boulevard bridge in Fort Lauderdale, we saw the Coral Ridge Towers where my mother lives and, just under the bridge, the Marine Office Building where my brother Bill keeps his law office.

The Marine Office Building is pretty unusual. First, there is a dock and a huge small-boat shed right on the waterway, and then built above it is a five or six story office building. Bill is very happy in one of the offices.

It was about ten o'clock Saturday morning, so I pulled alongside the docking area and popped upstairs to see if Bill was at the office.

No luck! I'll call him later when we get to our long-sought destination—Municipal Yacht Basin, New River, Fort Lauderdale, Florida.

As we pulled out of Bill's office docking area, we ran past my favorite waterway restaurant, Harrison's, a place where I had had many a lunch on the dockside patio as I watched other people run their boats up and down the waterway. Now it was my turn to return the waves of the diners. But alas, Harrison's was not open yet for lunch.

Under the Sunrise Boulevard Bridge we picked up famous Creighton's Restaurant and the Jordan Marsh sign on the right and all the gleaming glory of the Fort Lauderdale beach hotels on the easterly side.

Then it was under the Las Olas Boulevard bridge, a connector I had used so many hundreds of times, right up to and then past Bahia Mar, at one time the finest private yacht basin in the world and still excellent.

Either greed or poor planning, or perhaps both, had resulted in the shortsighted Fort Lauderdale City Fathers' filling and then leasing much of the superb yacht area to commercial ventures like a motel, restaurant, shops and parking. Fort Lauderdale lost part of her glittering tiara of Venetian diamonds when this happened not so many years ago.

A defender of this action once told me, "What the heck. It was good money for the city and no one will ever miss it."

They are wrong. I miss it, and I'm only one of millions. But much of the glamor remains. For instance, coming out of the area was *Hartline* out of Palm Beach, a monster of a yacht with plumes in her hair. For auxiliary transportation *Hartline* had sitting on her top deck a twenty-one-foot Boston Whaler Outrage plus a Datsun sedan, both boldly lettered *Hartline*.

Then, at the dock we saw *Blackhawk* out of Chicago, perhaps 100 feet or so, and as she had the insignia of the ice hockey Chicago Black Hawks emblazoned on her stack, I assumed this had to be the waterway plaything of the owner of the club—or maybe it belonged to the goaltender. At least it was an indication that these folks weren't really on relief.

"Look, Dad, there's Pier 66 and the tower with the revolving restaurant on top," exclaimed Carol. "Remember the time we went there?"

We remembered well, and this trip continued to be a thrill for all three of us—all children at heart.

Final Destination

We cruised under the bridge at the 17th Street Causeway, swung past Port Everglades to the mouth of the Port Everglades Inlet, took a picture of the great condominiums at Point of America.

We had arrived—gone as far south as we were going to go, this trip at least.

Carol gave the horn on *Islander* three booming blasts. The trip,

The banks of Fort Lauderdale's New River are always interesting.

about 1700 miles, was about over now and we would find our berth.

We swung *Islander* 180 degrees and came back past Chevron and Pier 66 and swung west, carefully picking our way into the mouth of the New River, a fine navigable stream that ran parallel with Las Olas Boulevard into the heart of Fort Lauderdale to the many boatyards beyond.

Carol, Patti and I marvelled at the great estates fronted on New River including one reported to be the present or past winter home of the Anheuser-Busch people, and I noted this with interest considering I am a consumer.

Then there were several other unusual homes, one with a cheery lawn sign that said to the boatsmen, "Hello there!" Another home had a huge glass window on the rear of the garage (or was it the living room?), and we could clearly see an antique auto on

The *Jungle Queen* squeezes her way up the New River several times a day.

display. My antique-buff friend John Reardon would have enjoyed this. A third home was on a point of land and had both a swimming pool as well as a full-size tennis court, plus a delightful lawn and barbeque area, all squeezed onto the lot.

Islander was moving ahead at four or five miles per hour as she moved around Tarpon Bend where New River became narrower and even more dramatically beautiful because the river now was teeming with action.

Cruisers carefully worked their way downstream in solitary single file as we moved carefully westward. The big Las Olas Boulevard sign was to our right. The old Stranahan Pioneer House came into view as we moved over the traffic tunnel which took the north-south traffic along Federal Highway.

Jackie waits at dockside as we arrive.

"Let's fill 'er up, Dad," says Jackie.

A Familiar Face

Someone on the right bank waved as *Islander* moved forward. He pulled into focus, still waving his left hand—bare to the waist, dungaree shorts, thick wavy hair.

"It's Jackie," screamed Carol as she recognized her brother, who was now working and living in Fort Lauderdale.

"Hi, Jack—how are you?" we all shouted.

"Welcome to Fort Lauderdale," he hollered back. "You're in Slip 174. Follow me."

Then he jumped in his tan Plymouth and slowly moved down New River Drive, waving out the window with his left hand as he drove.

We cruised along parallel with him and, as he pulled into a parking spot, I put our engine in neutral and started to get ready to take her into the slip.

Jackie caught our lines. We tied down in the space provided for us by Dockmaster Nelson Tetreault, formerly of Worcester, Massachusetts.

The cruise of the *Islander* was now over, and to this log I write "Finis."

Patti, Carol and Jackie.

My nieces Denise and Jaimie Conway help Carol wash down the decks at our New River berth.

Georgetown Marina from plane.

Typical traffic on waterway.